VOICES

from the Channel 4 Television series

WRITERS AND POLITICS

Umberto Eco	**Günter Grass**
Stuart Hall	**Salman Rushdie**
Nadine Gordimer	**Noam Chomsky**
Susan Sontag	**Fred Halliday**
E.P. Thompson	**Heinrich Böll**
George Konrad	**Kurt Vonnegut**

EDITED BY Bill Bourne, Udi Eichler and David Herman

SPOKESMAN
Nottingham: Atlantic Highlands

in association with
THE HOBO PRESS

LEABHARLANNA ATHA CLIATH
RATHMINES LIBRARY
ACC. NO.   0851 244939
COPY NO.   RR 1003
INV. NO.   4425
PRICE IR£   5.57
CLASS 320

First published in 1987 by:
Spokesman
Bertrand Russell House
Gamble Street
Nottingham, England
Tel. 0602 708318

and 171 First Avenue, Atlantic Highlands,
New Jersey 07716, USA
for The Hobo Press

Copyright © Brook Productions (1986) Ltd, 1987

This book is copyright under the Berne Convention. All rights
are reserved. Apart from any fair dealing for the purpose of
private study, research, criticism or review, as permitted
under the Copyright Act, 1956, no part of this publication may
be reproduced, stored in a retrieval system, or transmitted, in
any form or by any means, electronic, electrical, chemical,
mechanical, photocopying, recording or otherwise, without
the prior permission of the copyright owner. Enquiries should
be addressed to the publishers.

British Library Cataloguing in Publication Data

Writers and Politics. — (Voices).
1. Political science
I. Bourne, Bill   II. Eichler, Udi
III. Series
320   JA66

ISBN 0-85124-483-1
ISBN 0-85124-493-9 Pbk

Printed by the Russell Press Ltd, Nottingham
(Tel. 0602 784505)

0851 244939 1003

Lea

Dublin City Libraries
Rathmines Branch
Tel. No. 973539

WRITERS AND POLITICS

Books should b
Books (not alrea
application, by

Date Due

13 AU

20 ?

-3 F

SANTRY BOOKSTORE
DUBLIN CORPORATION PUBLIC LIBRARIES

Contents

Introduction

Voices is a television oddity. Apparently set in a late-night Oriental carpet warehouse, it attempts to present the most exciting debates going on in the world of ideas. The debates may be topical (The New Cold War, The Future of Work) or timeless (The Mind/Brain Argument). The important thing is that they matter and deserve to reach the large audience that only television can provide.

This means going into often new and foreign terrain. New because our world is rapidly changing. Issues like Artificial Intelligence and the Post-Industrial Society are now upon us, transforming the world we live in. Developments in computer technology pose real and disturbing questions about the mind and what it means to be human. This doesn't mean taking some 'Gee Wiz' attitude to the new, but to think through the changes and find the voices who can make sense of this newly emerging landscape.

The humanities too have undergone tremendous upheavals in the last 20 years: new ideas, new uncertainties and even new subjects. The language of literary critics and historians is sometimes barely recognisable and has moved away from our own common sense and everyday assumptions about writing or the past. There has been a revolution in the world of criticism, undermining our older assumptions about knowledge and the self. Increasingly it is here in the world of ideas rather than in the arts, that we sense 'The Shock of The New'.

Much of this shock is muffled by parochialism, distancing ourselves from new work by seeing it as faddish and foreign. Because so many of the great creative thinkers come from across the Atlantic or the Channel they lack any regular access to our review-pages or TV screens, and we tend to lose touch with the most important debates going on elsewhere. The important voices from abroad go unheard as if what they have to say doesn't matter. The results can be comical. When the British press finally caught up with Structuralist ideas during the row in the Cambridge English Department a few years ago, it was easy to forget that the theories at the centre of the controversy had been commonplace in Paris for 20 years. Despite the talk about 'The Global Village' intellectuals like

Chomsky or Levi-Straus remain strangers to our screens and their ideas remain at the margin of our culture. Even more extraordinary is how rare it is on British television to find discussion of the work of British intellectuals like Edward Thompson, John Berger and Raymond Williams. There is no obvious forum for the discussion of their ideas, at a time when British intellectual culture is in fact very rich.

This is part of a growing problem of communication. Our culture has created a huge gulf between its thinkers and the rest. We take this for granted in the more arcane reaches of science and mathematics, but the same is happening in literary criticism and history and the growing areas where science touches our lives. Both academics and media have been notoriously bad at communicating the main intellectual developments of our time to the rest of us, so that like Miss Havisham we continue to live in the past, surrounded by out-of-date theories and cobwebbed assumptions.

This in turn is partly a matter of categories. Some of these debates are neither Arts, Philosophy or Science in any clear sense, but slip in between established categories. When Umberto Eco and Stuart Hall talk about a pervasive sense of crisis — is that Current Affairs? Politics? History? When Cornelius Castoriadis and Chistopher Lasch talk about the breakdown of a sense of community or belonging they are not just talking about politics or sociology. These discussions are about culture in the largest sense, issues which speak to the heart of our experience, but which have no obvious home in the universities or the media.

Voices, then, tries to be alert to these problems, to this need for a forum where these kinds of issues can be discussed, and to follow an agenda which is being set by writers and intellectuals here and abroad. This agenda is often new and foreign, and may have no clear signposts. And even where there are signposts (Post-Structuralism, Post-Modernism) the question is what do they mean and why do they matter? That is perhaps a fancy way of saying: Who are the most interesting voices of our age and what do they have to say to us?

The dialogues that follow bring together a dozen leading writers and intellectuals to look at aspects of the postwar world. The series was broadcast in the summer of 1985, during the celebrations of the 40th anniversary of the end of World War II.

The War is the subject for the discussion between Heinrich Böll and Kurt Vonnegut. Böll was a German Prisoner of War on the Eastern Front, and Vonnegut was an American POW held in Dresden, where he witnessed the firebombing of the city, the subject of his famous novel *Slaughterhouse Five*.

Böll is one of the two great German novelists who have written about the need to confront the experience of Nazism. The other is Günter Grass, perhaps best known for *The Tin Drum,* who begins his dialogue with Salman Rushdie by discussing the impact of Germany's defeat on its language and literature and what it means to be a migrant in a century of migrants.

Perhaps the most decisive effect of the War on Europe has been the division of the continent between West and East. Forty years after the Yalta Conference, British historian E.P. Thompson discusses the future of Europe with one of East Europe's most distinguished writers, the Hungarian George Konrad.

The East/West conflict is also the subject for Noam Chomsky and Fred Halliday. Their argument about the nature of the continuing rivalry of the Superpowers leads them from Europe and 1945 to the New Cold War and conflicts in Latin America, Asia and Africa.

Politics is one of the key recurring themes in the series. Another is *Transition*, the idea of living through an interregnum, a time of change when traditional categories no longer describe our experience, while a new language is still struggling to be born. Umberto Eco — now famous for his novel 'The Name of the Rose'— and cultural critic Stuart Hall compare this sense of crisis in Italy and Britain, while South African novelist Nadime Gordimer and the American critic Susan Sontag look beyond Europe to the post-colonial world, to new emergent voices.

Voices has been a regular annual feature of Channel 4 since November 1982. The programme is made by Brook Productions and produced by Udi Eichler and David Herman.

CHAPTER 1

Crisis? What Crisis?

Umberto Eco and Stuart Hall

Umberto Eco is best known for his novel, the highly acclaimed *The Name of the Rose*, but in European intellectual circles he is renowned as a leading semiologist and and cultural critic, with books on every area of culture, from James Joyce to James Bond. Common to all Eco's work is a deep distrust of fanaticism and a belief in tolerance and rationalism. His values came under threat in Italy during the 1970s from the terrorism of neo-fascists and the Red Brigades. As in Germany, terrorism brought a deep sense of crisis, and this is the subject of Eco's latest book. Terrorism, he argued, is just one result of a more general crisis which began in the seventies, a crisis of European culture.

Like Eco, *Stuart Hall* is a leading cultural critic, interested in popular culture and new critical theory. But as a prominent figure in the New Left, his analysis is more political. He has been especially influential in recent debates about the state. Though Britain was spared the sense of crisis which terrorism brought to Italy in the mid-seventies, the summer riots of 1981 and the violence during the coal strike in 1985 have increased fears of a crisis of governability. But rather than a breakdown of law and order, Hall argues that Britain is more threatened by a slow drift towards authoritarianism. What Britain and Italy have in common, he believes, is not disorder but long-term economic change dividing both societies.

What Crisis?

Hall: I think the first thing to do is to establish what descriptively we mean when we talk about the sense of crisis. And I'll start by doing so against the British background. I mean, I have in mind sort of four dimensions. One is the economic one, which I start with because in a sense it's so obvious. Britain is in very serious trouble economically. Deindustrialisation is very far advanced. We're ceasing to be anywhere near the sort of forefront of economic development. I think clearly Britain has a particular problem here, but it's not one which Britain has alone. We're talking about that kind of trend throughout Western Europe, throughout the capitalist world in general. Secondly, the political one, and one could choose many instances here, but in Britain the most important sense that I have here is that there was a kind of consensus — I don't mean agreement, but a kind of sense of what the political conversation was about from about 1945 onwards — and that lasted, I think, in spite of the different rotation of governments and so on, and I have the sense that in the eighties that conversation has come to a stop and we're into another one, or trying to move into another one. And that's a huge lurch of the sort of taken-for-granted political expectations which underpin the culture.

I have another aspect of the political one which I'd love you to talk about, and that is a sense that I have of a growing gap between where people are politically and the institutions and organisations which express that in a sort of formal political way. I just feel that there's an enormous yawning gap between the parties and where their constituents are, how they imagine people feel politically and how they actually do feel etc. Well, that's a political dimension.

The third one's an ideological one. And here I'm talking really, I suppose, about on the Left. I mean, a sense of the crisis of the vocabularies which people have used classically to describe their situation and also to think about the future in. The absence of a model, classical models for change for the future. On the Right, on the other hand, a recovery of what I suppose feels to me like an extremely ancient language given an enormous new vitality for the 21st century. Adam Smith lives again is what one feels in Britain.

And the fourth dimension is the cultural one. It's the most complicated one of all to feel out, but there I have a strong sense of the deep underlying important cultural changes which have gone on which somehow we find it very difficult to give a name to, to identify in terms of a kind of consistent sequence and movement to see where they're pointing, and to feel certainly that political and economical forces are quite out of touch with modern culture. The drive of modern culture just doesn't find expression in the traditional forms in politics, in the way in which experts talk to us on television and so on. I see life somehow is moving to another rhythm. Well that's against an English background, I mean, are we talking about the same things in Italy?

Eco: Oh, I could say the same of Italy. But Stuart, I think that we have a duty to make some distinction about this curious notion of crisis. Maybe my standpoint is too much a continental *idesta speculative* but well, that's my function here. I think we have to distinguish between an objective crisis as a matter of fact and a crisis of our attitude toward crisis. Crisis is a moment of transition in which something that held before doesn't hold any longer and there is not yet something new. And in this sense crisis, biologically, physically, culturally speaking, is a permanent state. And I think that even in politics, in culture, that so-called state of crisis is always a positive state. Every new scientific discovery is a moment of crisis which destroys the previous world view. Social crisis arrives when people are unable to face this reality. Say Galileo Galilei discovers that the whole planetary system is different than we thought, that is a normal cultural crisis, a positive one. Epistomologists say it is a change of paradigm. The real social and cultural crisis is due to the fact that the culture of this time is unable to accept this challenge. So it would be interesting to see what in our time is, let me call it physiological crisis, and what is on the contrary our wrong, perverse way to respond to the crisis?

Hall: Well, I agree with a lot that you've said because I think that when people use the term they very often have in mind a kind of one-off seizure coming to them from outside. I mean, which is outside their volition and for which they have no responsibility, which doesn't involve them, etc. And it comes from outer space and it is a crisis. And I don't mean it in that sense, I mean it in your sense of the crisis occurring in terms of the capacity of the society to respond. Secondly, I think we have to recognise that societies can be in crisis for very long periods of time. We're talking about a process — but I just wonder whether you feel about the present situation that it is akin to a permanent state, or whether you think there's some features around just now, I suppose perhaps the number of places in the society in which the paradigms are collapsing? I mean, that might give one a special sense of urgency when, you know, in politics and economic life, in culture, in ideology and so on, when they all change at the same time without any common sense of direction, then people, I think, do begin to be panicked.

Eco: A permanent feature of modernity is the acceleration of the rhythm of crisis. In an ancient society you could live for three, four, five, six thousand years with the same social structure or the same kind of information. In a society like ours, that's so perfused with an exchange of information and contacts we have to learn how to live with a permanent state of crisis. But, you buy a personal computer, you spend a lot of money, you believe to have with you something that can solve all your problems. In the lapse of time from when you pay and they bring it to you, they have invented a new computer. That's a state of crisis. Because you would be obliged to change it, to shift immediately to the new. You have to learn how to cope with this situation of continuous uncertainty.

Let's try to speak of political crisis. We know that the generation of '68, in England and Great Britain like in Italy, like everywhere, at a certain point was disillusioned and they shifted toward drugs or terrorism or buddhism and oriental cults, herbalism, macrobiotics. The crisis had to be forecast. It was impossible that the kind of sudden instant revolution advocated by the movement of '68 was realisable. They thought of revolution as an instant coffee. The crisis had to arrive. But the social crisis of the generation is due to the inability of these people to accept a transformation of the situation in a positive way and the fact that many of them responded in a sort of escapist way. What they call the crisis of ideologies, a crisis of political commitment. So I am interested in these psychological, psycho-social aspects of the crisis, not in the fact that a certain project collapses. It collapses because it was a utopian project and all utopian projects are open to collapse.

Hall: Yes, but I mean isn't there a difference what phase of that cycle one is in? I mean, if you take '68 I quite agree with you that none of what was promised or forecast or looked forward to was likely to come at all or in the precise terms in which it was imagined or as rapidly as people imagined. The revolution tomorrow was not on the cards. Nevertheless, I can see what a positive crisis means in relation to '68. Because you see the disintegration of old modes of thought, of modes of feeling and modes of communication, but you see an enormous generation of positive starts. Some of them last, some of them are bound to lose themselves etc, but an enormous set of new possibilities coming into existence.

Eco: Absolutely right.

Hall: Now, that I think is the positive phase, and what I want to say about the present one is I feel differently about it when all of that has evaporated. That's to say, when the predominant feeling about the crisis is we have nothing new to say, the new initiatives are bound to run into the sands, we can't think the impossible or think the unthinkable. Because I think that that is a different phase, and you seem to me to take a kind of cyclical view of this, permanent crisis, permanent change, permanent uncertainty, so it doesn't matter very much whether one is in the upswing or the downswing of a crisis. And I think it does. I think we are now in the downswing.

Eco: We are, but my point is that the crisis is the crisis of a society which was unable to make a good computation of the positive and negative effects of something that happened. Take again '68, and in Italy '68 was not only the student confrontation of this dream of an instant revolution, it was a sort of generalisation of *la prise de la parole*, people that before were unable to speak up for themselves learned how to. Take a very traditional and Catholic society like the Italian one, between the seventies and the eighties there were two referendums, one on divorce and one on abortion, in which the majority of Italians said yes to divorce and yes to abortion. Ten years before it was absolutely inconcievable. So it means that the general atmosphere of '68 with all its negative, naive, savage aspects has produced a transformation of society. That's positive crisis. What's negative and produces the effects you analysed is now the attitude, not only of the young but also of the elders, to see historically everything that happened in '68 as a negative phenomenon without understanding how much the society has changed and to be able to decide what to plan from this point on. Instead of saying, well this has produced A, B and C, A is acceptable, B questionable, C negative — let's start from A and make a farther move, there is what in Italy is called 'reffluso' a sort of going back, reneging on everything that happened. And that's what I mean by crisis, the incapability of a society to recognise the real historical process and movement. My interpretation doesn't solve your problem. What you call a crisis still is there and we should maybe analyse it.

Hall: I suppose I'm really trying to pin down whether it's a difference between Italy and Britain. Because I very much agree with what you said about '68. When the smoke and fire cleared, what was impressive were the much deeper, slower, but really profound changes that had been, as you say, put on the agenda. Yes, and I think in Britain, of the kinds of things that you talked about, people who hadn't spoken before taking the word. A sense very much of changes in personal relationships and sexual mores etc. These deep underlying things of the culture really were shifted by '68. But my acute sense in Britain is that if I might call it, as it were, the enemies of all of that have never forgotten how much was unhinged in '68, and you could read in Britain the whole of the latter seventies and the eighties as an attempt specifically to liquidate it, to cancel it. And now I'm not sure that I would say that those things stand in the way in which you were describing them in Italy.

The Crisis of Reason

Eco: At this point I would like to insert the problem of the role of intellectuals, of culture. Two years ago I was invited to a meeting organised by the French government, gathering together scholars, writers from all over the world with this curious question, how can intelligentsia, how can culture help governments to solve crisis? And my intention was: 'just a moment, your duty is to solve your economical, social, urban, transportation, I don't know what, crisis, but the role of intellectuals is to produce crisis.' When John Locke writes an *Essay on Human Understanding* it produces a crisis within the English and the European culture, he discovers that according to reports of travellers there are different kinds of morals in different countries. That's a crisis. And it's a positive crisis. Probably while in '68 there was an idea of the militant role of culture as a sort of first rank green berets commando activity, now the role of culture is just of speculating about these up and down dialectics and to critically show in which way this sense of disillusion, this sense of impotence, can be reversed in a new starting point. Maybe it can take 10 years, in which a culture is no longer on the square, so to speak, politically. To reflect upon, to revisit, to make a re-reading of the records of the last 20 years. But maybe it is one of the ways which doesn't save the present generation from their disillusionment.

Hall: Don't you think that that is one of the forms of accommodation to the crisis? See, I mean isn't it extremely convenient when intellectuals impose on themselves this partial retirement from engagement? I don't mean that, you know, the only place to fight for ideas is on the barricades etc. I'm thinking you're quite right that intellectuals have an extremely important role precisely in that reflecting, for instance, in relation to '68, pointing back to what really remained after the heady promise was disintegrated. Intellectuals have that longer analytic function. But still they also have a function up front. And the point at which they're willing to retire from the scene and to leave the solution of the crisis to some other, to the political elite and to the economic power structures and to government, and simply themselves reflect on it, suits, it seems to me, the preservation of.. well it suits certain powers that be much better than others. It's a kind of self-imposed Socratic distancing, a sceptical distancing from the problems.

Eco: Well, you know, there is a book I like, Italo Calvino's *The Baron on the Trees* which is the story of this 18th century aristocrat who decides to spend all his life on the top of a tree without stepping down. But in doing that he participates, he takes part in the French revolution, in a lot of acts, critical moments of his era. He's an enlightened person. Well he's a metaphor, he's an allegory. But there is a way to stay up on the top of the tree and to change the life on the earth. But stop for a moment to describe the present crisis. Do you have an idea, do you have a project in which way you can overcome it, change the picture? Faced with a young man of the new generation in Great Britain who says 'well I don't trust any longer the student movements, I have been disillusioned by the Tories because it has proved to be so and so, I have no perspectives and so I abuse myself or I do something in which I don't believe so much, but let me wait because I have no immediate perspectives for the future.' what is the answer you think you can give?

Hall: Yeah, well, I can't give you one. At least I won't give you one straight off. But let me back off a little and come back, because, you see, I think you may have been taking me too literally when I talked about intellectual engagement. I don't mean necessarily, you know, the French situation where intellectuals have to be recruited directly into governments etc. Or even where their statements have to be explicitly political. Because I agree with your earlier analysis, namely that the crisis isn't only the crisis of those most immediate structures. We use the term because it's also the longer, deeper paradigms of feeling and understanding which have cracked and disintegrated. And intellectuals, it seems to me, do have some responsibilities, particular responsibilities at that level too. So it's not an immediate engagement. So what I would — in answer to your question — would not be to unroll an immediate solution to the crisis in a simple way, but to talk about the problem of your young person. Now, let's think about that for a moment because it seems to me in the past we have always thought, on the Left, say, that of course one wasn't simply analysing the society in a kind of religious way in which nothing changed. One was trying to bring to bear one's analytic schemes against the changes in history which are going on in front of our eyes. But all the same there was a sense that the new and emergent forces were not wholly unintelligible in terms of the schemas that we'd had before. So you had a constant movement. You take the new evidence and you rework the old ideas and renovate them and there's an active kind of dialectic going on between them. Whereas now, I think if you talk about that sense of disillusionment it is a very profound one indeed.

It is, to caricature it only a little, none of the languages have anything to say. Socialism is, you know, ancient. We know of no possible models that would come anywhere near what we want. We are beyond rationalism and rational definition of ends and means. All those languages are not just in difficulties but there's a sense that they're totally collapsed. Now, the total collapse of the basic paradigms of a culture like that is an extremely difficult situation to see any movement out of because you don't know what the new is in dialogue with. The new has to be in dialogue with something which you are modifying to change, to take into account. Now, what I want to ask you is is that an illusion? Is it an illusion to say that? Of course those models are in crisis, but in what sense has rationalism collapsed? I mean, has that paradigm gone? Is the talk of post-modernism, you know, post-everything, we are in the post-everything — I mean, I don't know how to think about the future in a society in which people say to me 'we are post-everything.'

Eco: And I am frightened by the new upheaval of irrationalism. Recently in Italy as well as in France there were many debates about the crisis of reason. And at this point we have to teach people that reason, rationality is not an absolute value, it is a technique, a conjectural activity. In Italy some of my friends have launched a new slogan of the 'weak thought' against the 'strong thought' of the old rationalism, a weak conjectural thought able to correct itself.

That is a notion of reasonability, if I can coin this term, that has to be taught — '68, in a way, was still bound to a mythical notion of reason, even Marxism. It was the not representative of universal reason. The disillusionment of the young generation comes just because they maybe believe too strongly the ideal of reason and are unable to accept this more human notion of reasonability. And I think that to speak in favour of that, to explain that the alternative is not between reason and irratonalism but there is a middle way, is a political task.

Twenty years ago you couldn't teach in a university if you didn't accept a discussion of the hot issues, of political issues. I did it, as everybody did it. Somebody did it too much. I remember that in '68 I told the students, 'you want to make the revolution, okay. But in the new world you need somebody who is able to drive airplanes, otherwise the airplanes will always be driven by the other people, so you have also to understand how the engine of an airplane works even though it doesn't look to you revolutionary enough, you have to learn mechanics.' And the attitude of the students at that time was 'no, mechanics is a capitalistic trick.' Then the new generation, on the contrary, now is in the university only in order to understand how to drive an airplane. But now the function of a teacher is maybe to reinsert this kind of knowhow into the framework of the moral perspective of the more long-term view. So, curiously enough, if my role in '68 was to speak in favour of mechanics, now it is to speak against. But I think this is a political role. In a moment in which your students would ignore absolutely the political destiny of what they are learning and planning to do. I don't see it as *diminutzio capitis*, a reduction of my role, I recognise it as my political role in a moment of transition.

Hall: Well, I think I agree with you. But I want to probe it a bit because I think, for instance, on the Left that the dream of having some single explanatory system, whether that is Marxist or.. you know, the economic forces drive everything else etc, so patently does not describe the world around us, and especially does not describe the world as everybody lives it, including the people who subscribe to these theories, that we have to think, what on earth can one use as, as you say, political tools for analysing your situation? And there it seems to me an immense positive gain in the recognition of difference, of diversity, of heterogeneity. You know, of the different range of things that move people to action. Of the different kinds of contradictions in complicated societies like ours. The notion that people do not have single ideas that they're ascribed to have. The working class does not have the the great idea it was supposed to have, etc. That seems to me difficult. And obviously it puts a whole number of relations and institutions of the labour movement and the Left in crisis, but actually it is, I think, a positive escape from a kind of prison house of thought. So I think that is very positive.

But let me try and put my problem about that and taking that formal thinking right to the very end. Because you see, in each sphere in which this disintegration, this necessity for the recognition of diversity occurs, I still see problems, enormous problems affecting vast numbers of people each day in their everyday lives, not just as a matter of intellectual conception, but as it's lived. Problems which are in a sense extremely old but which nevertheless are there. The question of poverty. The question of the unequal access to this diversity, this rich diversity we're talking about. The question of the discrepancy between advanced and non-advanced peoples. The real problems of empowering the vast numbers of the disorganised and the powerless who could now, given the means of doing so, actually begin to exercise judgement and choice in the spheres that count, but who are excluded from power. Now these are in a sense ancient, they're questions that have always been with us, to which the great philosophers attempted to give a kind of answer. What we are saying is that some of those answers are incorrect in their certainties and their abilities to command the whole terrain of the problem, but the problems themselves don't disappear.

*Eco:*Yes, but Stuart maybe we risk mixing up the cultural response to crisis with the political response to crisis. I was mentioning this meeting in Paris in which I said, 'you politicians, in so far as you are politicians, you have to solve crisis. We intellectuals, in so far as we are intellectuals, we have to create them.' This doesn't mean that myself as an intellectual I'm not obliged to take on the political position. Sometimes the role of the philosopher, of the sociologist, is to say 'in this moment there is no global answer to that problem because the answers you presented as global were not such.' That doesn't mean that there is no political answer, no local intervention.

The Construction of Crisis

Hall: But look, to go back to where the conversation started, what then ought we to say about crisis? I mean should we warn about the positive and negative potentialities which crises have? Should we draw attention principally to the way in which those crises have been misunderstood, been understood as sort of temporary phenomena which are going to go away and the certainties will return and one is not in that rhythm any longer, one is in the rhythm of perpetual change etc? Or do we have a duty to look at the way in which the crisis is itself constructed in public consciousness? Because, I mean, that's very important.

Eco: The way in which also false images of crisis are produced?

Hall: Yes. We have had, you see, for a time the analysis in Britain was that there is no crisis at all, it's all a smoke screen and the term ought not to be used etc etc etc. Now, and interestingly coming from quite the opposite side, it is the Right that say of course you're in crisis, we've been in crisis since 1945 and what has been going on is a failure to recognise the depth of the crisis and therefore to square up to the very hard medicine. You know, you have to take on the new realism in order to understand what is going on. But there's another area of displacement which is very common in Britain and that has been the displacement of crisis onto the enemy within. That is the notion that, as it were, what is happening is a kind of general breakdown of society and that one of the main people responsible for that is precisely the intellectuals. Precisely, you know, critical intellectuals because they have fed and nourished this destruction of the standards, the traditions, etc. We are the enemies, the kind of secret enemies of order, and the attempt then to connect this sense of disquiet with the most conservative of responses. I mean, essentially the response to be protected from change, protected from this knowledge about diversity, and to reach for certainty through imposing something on society. That is really the source of what I would call a kind of authoritarianism. When you say the word nowadays people immediately say 'well, do you think we're about to become fascist?', and of course the whole point about it is that it isn't like that, it preserves the existing system perfectly intact. Parliament, representation, you know, these are the things we want, these are our traditions. So it doesn't intend to disrupt the facade of political and social life at all, but behind it, it really wants to kind of restore those old certainties. Now that displacement of politics into law and order, into the fear of the enemy within and the collapse of social order has a resonance amongst, and mobilises, some of the most conservative elements. And by that I don't just mean conservative people, but I mean it speaks to the conservative element in all of us, you know, that fear of change, the fear of difference.

Eco: Well, we feel it in Italy at this moment because in order to react to terrorism Italian society has criminalised their whole past, the whole '68. Even people that in '68 were participating, taking part in rallies, now it is like they never never took part. And this is a sort of activity in which the intellectuals' speculative duty coincided with the political duty to make it clear, to deconstruct the hysteria. That's important. Crisis can be manoeuvred by power in order to keep you quiet, and the political duty is maybe also to make an analysis of the notion of crisis, as this evening we tried roughly to do, pay attention, don't believe that crisis is a sort of massive object.

There are different kinds of crisis. You have to distinguish between them. Take the interesting case at the moment of law and order establishment, the so-called new American patriotism. Flags everywhere, a new national pride. There has been, I don't remember where, an analysis of this attitude in which it was shown that the construction of this new feeling was a very artificial construction by which the Americans were proud to be proud of themselves. That there was no real substance behind the pride, but the pride was the pride of the pride. Well, unfortunately the analysis passed over the heads of the public because it is a kind of analysis we have the duty to make at every moment, to show, because we speak of the end of ideologies. Ideologies never end, they simply substitute each other. The end of an ideology means the rise of another. And maybe we have also the duty to say what is an ideology? In my opinion since ideology can be taken in a sort of a Che Guevara-like enthusiasm as a positive weapon or as a negative corruption, the ideology is the opinion of my adversary. Ideology is a system of beliefs which is so closed that it doesn't leave a place for the self-contradiction and for the recognition of alternative systems of belief. Certain ideologies, since they were too closed collapsed. And there is the big lie of the end of ideology while on the contrary we are living under the standard of new ideologies and the demystification, the analysis of those new ideologies can be an important task.

Hall: Which is one of the reasons why early in the conversation I was trying to rescue some notion of rationality or reasonability. Because you see, I'm again speaking about the British context, but in one sense you could analyse the crisis in the most obvious objective terms. You could look at the economic trends, yes, deindustrialisaton, you could look at the break-up and the new class and social formations or you could look at the crisis in the existing political institutions. In another way, you could give an account of the crisis entirely from what might be thought by many people to be non-political points of view. You could take crime. You could take a sense of being British. The sense of national identity. You could take this question that you raised before of patriotism, of the recrudescence since the Falklands of a deep but narrow vein of English patriotism. You could take this, what I was talking about before, this kind of lust for order. It's almost a need for the society to be disciplined. If it accepts the line that since '68 we have been, you know, doing what the British hate, freeing ourselves, entering pleasure, recognition of our desires and so on. And in England, you know, one bad winter must be followed by a period of self-punishment, and so we are going through that. So the more Mrs Thatcher asks us to eat bitter pills the better we feel. The bracing the back, stiffening the lip. Well the abilities for the crisis to kind of connect with those areas of masochism, with that thirst for authoritarianism, which comes from below; if it only came from above, from the existing state and the centres of power, we would know what to do with it, but it's when it's able to translate itself into a popular idiom of feeling, when people really are afraid and they do see the fact that their streets are changed because there are black people living there, it doesn't look how it looked in their childhood, and people speaking different languages or playing the wrong kind of music or loving one another in the wrong way, you know, they feel their whole world has kind of shifted on them. And when that fusion is made from one kind of crisis from above to a sense of the crisis which is being constructed from below, one has a very, very deep movement in the direction of irrationalism. And it seems to me against that, though we no longer believe in the great Reason, in the singular, or in the 'reason' that we used to give ourselves for everything, we do have to affirm the ability to critically interrogate those deep irrational fears because the crisis feeds on them in our society.

Eco: And to be able to show how many times what we believed to be realities or values are a linguistic problem. Sometimes it's a very political gesture to say what you are doing is the effect of a purely linguistic strategy and you are making us believe that there is a thing beneath it, while there is nothing. I believe that at a certain point it can be sometimes — not always, not regularly — a political duty to say 'I refuse this political discourse because it's false. Don't try to involve me in these games. For the moment I remain outside, let's say instead of engaging myself in that political discourse I prefer to work in the school, in the university or writing for a newspaper.' But there is an old term in Italy which is *Qualunquismo*, like the French Poujardisme, which is ' I am not concerned with politics'. But what I am saying now is not *Qualunquismo*, it's a way to act politically by saying ' this is not a real political issue. I won't take part in that discussion because I contributed to the mystification of the situation.'

Hall: We've refused then, I think rightly, to suggest that there is a kind of either single or an obvious set of answers or new paradigms to the kind of problems of crisis we've been discussing. I think it wouldn't be right though to leave the topic without trying to say what our own subjective take on that is. So let me say my piece and see what you think of it. I am torn between what I see as the positive advantages of this recognition of diversity and change, because — you know, people talk about Marxism — the only Marxism worthwhile is the Marxism that is not guaranteed by any abstract laws. The only paradigms which really can catch the contradictoriness of current change etc. Any other is, I think, increasingly, a kind of displaced desire for religion, it's a desire for certainty, for faith, for absolute guarantees. And I think that era is over and I think from the Left we've got to welcome that. I feel the positive advantage of the way in which the break-up can in fact lead us to construct more adequate ways of understanding, gradually put together more adequate kinds of politics. At the same time I suppose I am torn by a more pessimistic, more immediately pessimistic feeling, because I think that while that longer reconstruction is going on the existing centres of power are very much in command, setting the agenda, structuring the field. I mean, I think they are engaged in as radical a shoring up of the existing structures as we are talking about a radical disintegration of them. And I think that leaves untouched and untouchable such central issues as the alienation of work and the questions I talked about before, poverty, unemployment, the collapse of skills, the disintegration of communities etc, even the restoration of old standards, of old images of what it is like to be men and women etc which really belong to a hundred years ago and define political and economic forces reinforcing those sort of things, putting them back in place. In that sense, I think, very much kind of undoing what they imagined '68 set in train. I think those forces are very powerful, I think they command the stage, and I don't know whether they're going to allow us the time for a more open-ended, contingent kind of critical stance. So that's why I'm torn between a kind of pessimistic and optimistic view of what the crisis offers us.

Eco: I could answer only in a religious way. I had a religious education then I abandoned it, but I remember in my youth I was highly influenced by the French writer Emmanuel Mounier, who was speaking of *'optimisme tragique'*, tragic optimism. You know that life is a tale told by a idiot, full of sound and fury, and so on and so forth, but you have always a certain hope to keep going to do something. The only problem is what would you do if you knew that the world will be blown up tomorrow? I think that people can be divided into two great categories. The ones who say 'well I will kill myself, I will go to sleep, I will take some pills,' and the others who say 'no, I shall write my last article. I shall carve my last statue, I shall make my last gesture of compassion because, who knows, maybe a small satelite will survive with that article, with that statue, with the memory of that gesture, and let's see what happens.' I know it's only a sort of mystic response, even though in a secular mood, but the idea of a tragic optimism seems to me better than the one of an optimistic tragedy.

Hall: Yes, I mean it's somewhere between those alternatives isn't it? I don't see that our conversation could end anywhere else.

Eco: We're not oracles.

Hall: No certainly not, and it's not only that it seems that we've lost the belief that oracularism, to coin a phrase, is what intellectuals ought to be into now and that is, I think registering that passage, that transition is a very profound one. After that it's a kind of optimism of the will, or pessimism of the intellect as Gramsci said, but I've enjoyed talking to you.

Eco: Me too, Stuart.

CHAPTER 2

Writers and Politics

Nadine Gordimer and Susan Sontag

Nadine Gordimer is the highly acclaimed author of eight novels and more than a hundred short stories which reflect the painful conflicts and injustice of her native South Africa. Her writing is distinguished from that of other critics of apartheid by her ability to marry a European literary sensibility with a strong moral voice, and this has led to the banning of several of her books.

'The tension between standing apart and being fully involved; that is what makes a writer.' *Selected Stories*

In recent years she has become increasingly troubled by the divided loyalties of the writer — namely, responsibility and commitment to her society, on the one hand, and to literary values and integrity on the other.

For 20 years, *Susan Sontag* has been one of the most influential cultural critics in America, coming to prominence as a polemical champion of the avant garde aesthetic of the sixties. She has written prolifically about the major themes and figures of contemporary modernism, often focusing on the darker face of modern culture: pornography, the aesthetics of fascism and the extremism of the avant garde.

'A work of art, so far as it it a work of art, cannot... advocate anything at all. *On Style*

In the 'sixties, Susan Sontag's interest in modern art as essentailly radical and subversive went together with a political radicalism. She has since become increasingly disillusioned with the revolutionary left and more resistant to the claims that politics and society make on the artist.

Being Called to Account

Gordimer: You know, Susan, when I first began to write, as a child — I began when I was about nine years old; I had wanted really to be a dancer, and then, for various reasons, I could see that wasn't going to work out — I was writing for myself. And I could never have dreamed, even when years went by and I kept on writing and I was in my early teens and I'd even published — at 15 I published my first short story — I would have never have dreamed that this dark and wonderful and mysterious secret, which was the wish, the will and the wish to make with words — fascinated with words and how they could be used to express what I was taking in from the life around me and from my inner life — I would never have dreamed that this would become work for which I would be taken to account by anybody. I never dreamed that it was an act of responsibility to write.

Sontag: Had you seen yourself as having an audience, as writing for other people, or simply for yourself?

Gordimer: I think I saw it as writing for myself. And it came out of reading, of course. It came out of the fact that books, other people's books, were my life. And the discovery that I perhaps could make with words myself was something extraordinary, though I didn't ever think of being published and I didn't think of anybody else reading what I wrote. How did you begin?

Sontag: I had a different experience. I also began when I was seven, I think, seven or eight, I started to write stories, plays, poems. It was entirely inspired by other people's books. If I read a play and then I wanted to write a play, I read poetry, I wanted to write poetry, I read stories, I wanted to write stories. But I did think of being published. In fact, I really thought that that's what being a writer was. I also had no idea of what the responsibility of being a writer was, but I imagined that I would become a series of books. And what I thought writers were, were their books. I couldn't imagine what a writer's life was, but on the other hand, I couldn't imagine writing without it ending up in a book. But that too was an absolutely private experience.

Gordimer: In my case, being born in a country like South Africa, white, automatically privileged, living, brought up in the colonial life, as I was, if I was going to be a writer there would have to be a time when I would see what was in that society, when I would see how it had shaped me and my thinking and that I would bear, automatically, a certain responsibility for it as a human being. And since a writer is an articulate human being, there would be a special responsibility to respond to it in a certain way.

But, you know, I was reading Rilke and Virginia Woolf and Henry James and Proust, not when I was nine years old, but when I was 15-16, so there was a kind of blindness in me. I simply thought, 'well, I'm writing, it's the one thing in the world that I want to do.' I bathed myself in it. And it seemed to me entirely my affair that it was concerned with my inner feelings, with my responses, sensuous responses mainly at the beginning, to the world around me.

And then later on, also in my teens, it came to ethical questions, how to live? I was brought up without any formal religion of any kind, so I didn't have any of that structure around my life and I think that I was looking for that personal structure subconsciously through my writing. I was trying to make sense of what life was about through my writing.

Sontag: But I don't think you were hiding when you were reading Proust and Henry James and Tolstoy and Dostoyevsky. You were seeking your essential identity as a writer, which was to be part of literature; and literature is for us, certainly, at the end of the 20th century, an international activity. No serious writer, I would dare say, can afford only to know the literature of his or her own country, or his or her own language.

So in what sense were you hiding? You were seeking what would make you a writer, and at the same time you were coming to an awareness of what it means to be a citizen of your country. But I don't think that you were mistaken in reading those writers and attaching yourself to those writers, because that's what's made you the writer you are, that you cared about Proust and Henry James, and not, if I can jump ahead, taking your models from African literature, for instance, because you wanted to assume some relation to the problem of being an African, or in particular, being a white African, a white South African.

Gordimer: No, no, I'm not suggesting that I was following the wrong path. What I'm saying is I was doing and feeling what you felt. I wanted to write well. What I was seeking was excellence. I was seeking my own way of expressing the world that I knew as a writer.

Sontag: And why is that different from what you do now?

Gordimer: Well, the political aspect is something that came into my work implicitly, because the life around me was imbued with it, even the most private aspects of life were penetrated by the effects of politics. Politics wasn't and isn't something that you just choose to be involved in in South Africa. The political climate, the social order, the way you live, is determined by politics without any question of choice coming into it. But what I didn't understand, what I felt this kind of innocence about, was that as a writer I thought that — when I grew up and I became aware of where I was living and of my responsibilities as a human being, as a citizen — I saw it as something completely separate from what I was doing as a writer.

And even when political situations determined the lives of the characters in my books, because that was happening all around me, I still saw it as part of what I was making, in terms of literature. And the challenge was to make it well. It had nothing to do with whether I was satisfying people who shared my political opinions.

Then there came a time when I was called to account for the attitudes revealed by the characters in my books. This is what I am

talking about. Then to my surprise, I discovered that other people
didn't see me as a citizen as one entity, and myself as a writer as
another, to be left alone, not to be questioned as to how she was
employing her sensibility.

Sontag: At what point do you think you began to think of yourself
in this way? I don't see such an evolution in your work, but you
obviously do feel that there was a moment in which you had a sense
of yourself as a public person, as a writer, that you did not have
earlier when you first started to write.

Gordimer: I'll give you an example: in my last book of stories
there's a story which concerns a black woman who is a traitor,
really. Her husband brings back a black man on the run and she
seems to put up with him perfectly, she feeds him and conceals him
from the neighbours for a week or two. And then one Sunday
afternoon she just walks out to the police and gives him up. Well, I
hope that in the story I've shown why this could be, but if you look
at the situation baldly, I have shown a black woman who has
betrayed the struggle.

A black writer friend has said to me, 'never mind whether the
story works or not, whether it's a good story or not, you shouldn't
have written this about one of our sisters. We're all in the struggle
together.' But I said these things happen. I've written stories about
whites where the same kind of thing happens, because betrayal is in
the air in South Africa. It's natural, wherever there's a tremendous
political struggle going on there are always many informers, and this
is part of the climate of strange suspicion and distress in which we
live, even sometimes among intimates the word goes round that so-
and-so isn't to be trusted any more.

Sontag: But why didn't you say to them 'I am describing people. I
am giving a voice to people.' I mean, Chekhov, for instance,
always, all his life — I know he's a writer that both of us admire to
the point of adoration — Chekhov said that the writer's main
relation to politics should be one of flight and that you should never
allow yourself to become captured by other people's demands that
you express a progressive point of view. Chekhov said, 'all I worry
about is that I do justice to the reality of my characters'. Why
couldn't you answer those people in South Africa who were saying,
'well, you give expression to this point of view'. Well, 'yes, you do',
you say, 'because these are people who really exist'. This is the
reality of the society. You can't not write about it, because it is the
reality of your society. But it doesn't mean that you are taking a
position necessarily in your work.

Gordimer: No, but you see, at the time when this kind of
questioning came up — and it also came up at the time when I was
first beginning to mix with black people as equals — that would be

blacks who were beginning to write, who were acting, some black journalists, musicians — when I began to realise that it wasn't just enough to say, 'well, I'm a writer, that's what I do, and this is a very private activity.' And I didn't have the confidence then to bring forward the argument that you have, with which I agree. I would certainly agree with Chekhov rather than with Albert Camus who said 'the day when I cease to be no more than a writer, or only a writer, I shall not be a writer any more.' I disagree with that entirely. I would turn it round the other way. The day when it's more important for me to be more than a writer, in the public sense, in the sense of being answerable to some political or social problem in which I may be very involved as a citizen, the day that that becomes more important than being a writer, I think I'm discounted in the world. I have got no use and no place, because I believe that you must do the thing you do best. And if you're a writer it's a mistake to become then a politician, even though you believe passionately in a particular cause.

Sontag: But I don't see why you think writing is private in that sense. I mean, writing is solitary. You do it alone. And it is perhaps the most solitary occupation there is, certainly of all the arts, because even painters, though normally one painter paints a canvas, but it's still quite common for a painter to have assistants around, mixing the paints or taking care of the studio or answering the telephone or something. But most writers would find it utterly unbearable to have anyone else around when the writing is being done. So it is indeed the most solitary of all arts and we all complain and feel very sorry for ourselves that we have to stay cooped up all day long every day and can't go out and play like other people. But it's not private. It's simply work done in private. But I never think of the activity of the writer as a private activity, and I think even the.. Joyce fled Ireland, and that meant that he fled a certain kind of overt political involvement that he might have had to have if he'd remained in Dublin, and he cut himself off and he became a professional foreigner.

Gordimer: Silence, cunning and exile?

Sontag: Yes, and yet his work has mattered, I would say, even politically. It certainly is a public gesture, however private a person Joyce became by going into exile and living in Trieste and France and Zurich, and so forth. You see, I think that the writer, by the writer choosing to write — obviously I mean the good writer, I'm not just talking about writers as a social category, but someone who produces good writing and who is part of literature — is always making something social in standing for excellence, standing for a certain hierarchy of values protecting the language which is the thing that ultimately all writers — that's our medium and we want to prevent it from decaying or deteriorating.

We want to leave the language in perhaps slightly better shape because of our passage through it in all our books rather than in worse shape. The writer stands for singularity. The writer stands for an individual voice. The existence of good writing stands for an independent or autonomous life, or self-reliance. These are all public, civic, moral values that don't necessarily involve the kind of communal, civic engagement that you are talking about, which I understand perfectly. I don't live in a country where I very often feel absolutely called on to take a public position. I've taken a lot of public positions in my life, but I always felt that I volunteered to do it. I stuck my neck out, often the consequences were rather unpleasant.

Gordimer: I want to ask you, then, why you did that. You had choice. Why did you get so involved, for instance, in the Vietnam war and put a lot of creative energy into writing about it and perhaps speaking on public platforms? It would have belonged to your theory, and mine, that the thing that comes first is the striving for excellence as a writer. The fidelity to the word. You too must have felt this responsibility, this demand upon you. Why? Because you were an articulate person, a person of certain views, of Left views? Did you feel compelled then to leave your real work and do this?

Sontag: I think I felt compelled first of all as a human being and not as a writer. That is to say, I felt that it was a privilege to be a writer, that I had a privileged situation in the society and that I had a public voice and that there was an emergency in which I felt I could use my voice to influence people for something that I cared passionately about, but as a human being and as a citizen, as an American citizen, was horrified by the actions of my government. And when I and other writers came up, that had an impact because we were public figures.

I ended up, in fact, writing a book, a small book called *Trip to Hanoi*, but as you remember in that book, I started by saying that I had accepted an invitation from the North Vietnamese government to visit North Vietnam as a reward for all the public speaking and getting arrested and whatnot that I had done for a couple of years in the United States. But I went with the firm resolve not to write another one of those books that you write when you go to a country, about their wonderful revolution and so on. And I ended up writing it. But I began my book by saying that I hadn't wanted to write it, and I think my little book shows throughout the kind of ambivalence I felt about fulfilling that traditional modern ethical task of the writer, which is to be an opponent of state power, to be an opponent of oppression, to defend oppressed minorities. I mean, I think it's rather a modern definition of the writer, let's say since

Voltaire, since the French Enlightenment, one of the last 200 years. I think it's part of what it is in modern life to be a writer, that many of us think we have an ethical responsibility, but I don't think it's what determines our value as writers.

Gordimer: No, but you have just, in what you've been saying now, defining the necessity you felt to put yourself at the service for your society as a public figure, which is indeed a demand upon you, because you were articulate, because you were well-known as a writer. So then, your society wants you to be something else, so it is exactly the same kind of demand that is made on somebody like myself, only in my situation, it is much stronger because I am living in the midst of suffering and seeing the oppression of black people around me. I've lived in the middle of it ever since I opened my eyes there, in my privileged white hospital where I was born, where no black child could be born. And if I die there, I would be buried in a white graveyard where no black is allowed to be buried. So it is literally a cradle to the grave situation of having the unnatural and oppressive social order around you every minute of your life, so the responsibility is staring you in the face as a human being.

Sontag: But to what extent do you think your work is consecrated to exploring this oppression and this injustice? Do you feel that you have a necessary subject? I know a lot of writers in the United States who secretly envy writers who are born in Central or Eastern Europe, or countries that live under Soviet tyranny or someone from South Africa — you in particular, since you are the great South African writer — or the writers who come from countries in Latin America which have Rightwing dictatorships, I know many American writers who say, 'oh, if only we had a situation that we could so clearly define as one of oppression, where we had a necessary subject matter, such as someone from South Africa or Poland or Chile might have.' I don't share this view and I think it would be frivolous to envy people their historical tragedies.

But you must know for most American writers it isn't so obvious what we ought to talk about, what we ought to write about, even though none of us, I think, with any sense would claim that there aren't tremendous problems of justice and injustice in America. But practically no American writers feel that that should be their principal subject in the way that that subject of oppression, of justice, seems so self-evident if you come from a very vicious dictatorship or racist society.

Gordimer: Well, I don't feel consecrated to that subject at all. You know, I almost had to interrupt you then, because it alarms me to think that I should feel myself consecrated to a problem, a racial problem or a problem of social justice, even though it impinges very much upon my life, my thought and everything else, and though I care deeply about it and I feel responsible for it. Anybody who's born there bears responsibility for it.

Sontag: But Nadine, you said more than that. You said that it is actually part of everyone's life and consciousness. therefore, in so far as your stories are principally set in South Africa, and they are, your novels, there is no way in which, let's say you could write a novel about surburban adultery in the style of John Updike and the fact of apartheid, the separation of the races, the oppression of black people in South Africa, would not somehow enter in, if only let's say in the interplay between servants and employers in the household being described.

Gordimer: Well, you see, that is what I'm always at pains to try and explain to people. I don't choose apartheid as a subject, or oppression as a subject. I don't go out and look for it. I am what I was when I began to write at nine years old. I write about what I know and feel and see and what I absorb from the life I live and the life around me. And it happens to be, in that country, with what is happening there. Just as if I were Gabriel Garcia Marquez, I would be writing out of the heart of that society, as he does. It's simply, it's the air I breath and the food I eat. It's the bus I get on, it's the cinema I go to, the library I use. My whole life is implicit with it, and so it comes naturally into my writing. It seeks me out, I don't seek it.

Looking for a Subject

Sontag: Having a subject, and the relation to the subject, I think is for serious writers a much less innocent relation than it used to be. To portray one's society and the panorama of human folly and frailty, I think it was much easier to define in the time of, say, Thackeray or Balzac or any of the great Russian novelists than it is for us. On the whole, the writers who clearly have subjects in the traditional sense are kitsch writers, they're entertainment writers, they're not part of literature. Whereas most of the major writers, I think, of the last few generations — and you can take this all the way back to Flaubert, who's our original ancestor — but most of the great achievements of 20th century literature, seem to make a claim to be beyond the subject, to be self-referential, to be ultimately about language and about sensibility. If you think of Joyce or Virginia Woolf, for example, two great figures of British literature, I think that what is interesting for someone who doesn't come from a society in the throes of a racist dictatorship, or living under great oppression, or in the beginning of a revolutionary process, what is fascinating to, say, a Western European or North American, is to think that you can be like yourself, Nadime, a modernist writer and a writer with a great subject if you come from Eastern or Central Europe, if you come from Latin America, if you come from a country like South Africa. Whereas I think American writers, on the whole, do not feel really serious writers. The writers I admire most in the United States don't feel the necessity of a subject. You can be a modernist and have a great subject, and I think that's where you are in a somewhat different situation historically than an American writer or a British writer, or a French or German writer.

Gordimer: I think, what has happened now with writers, for instance, like Milan Kundera, to a certain extent myself, the two coincide, it's showing that it's possible for the inner landscape and the outer landscape to become one, to meld together in the same work. In other words, the inner landscape, which is really the subject of the novel, the techniques, the sensibilities, the perceptions for that, can be used, even the technical side can be used with the outer landscape, the subject.

I find it very strange that to my mind, as a stranger in Europe, a stranger in America, with the curious fact that I'm not a stranger in the language, I belong to the guild of the language, that I share not only with the writers but with other people here and therefore, obviously, the culture that goes along with the language to a certain extent. I find it amazing that British writers seem to avoid that outer landscape almost completely. I wonder now, when, in 1984 there was this long miners' strike — it must have affected the lives of so many people living in the areas where the mines are, it must have changed their whole lives for a very long time — I just wonder whether any novels, any stories, are going to come out of this, any fiction's going to come out. Or is it only going to be recorded in the press and in television?

Sontag: I don't think that I want novels to bring me news. I think I look to the higher journalism and to essays, and to film, to a certain kind of film essays which I think are very important, to give me a sense of how sensibility is altering under the pressure of immediate events. What I want from fiction, well I think the writer is a conjurer, and I think I want a certain kind of magic, a certain kind of delight. I want my sense of the language reinforced and I want my sensibility modified in some way. I want my sympathies enlarged. But they might be enlarged by the study of what you would, I think, describe as a private situation. You see, I'm not so sure that the private and the public can be described in this way. I know that modern English literature is very often viewed, let's say, as a quarrel between sort of formalist critics on the one hand and Leavisites on the other hand. Or among writers, let's say, Virginia Woolf on the one hand, Orwell on the other hand. That Virginia Woolf stands for the kind of private writer, writer of sensibility, and

Orwell for the responsible public writer, public figure. But I think that Virginia Woolfe was.. her work is full of ideas about the public realm.

Gordimer: Ah, but there you are.

Sontag: But she's being true to herself and her perceptions of the world by, describing, largely.. well *Mrs Dalloway* is about a woman giving a dinner party.

Gordimer: To the Lighthouse is about an expedition that doesn't come off.

Sontag: A family, a moment in the life of a family, but there is a whole society portrayed there. And if Virginia Woolf had views, let's say the feminist views that are expressed in *Three Guineas* and *A Room of One's Own*, I'm glad that she used the essay to give voice to those views, but I don't expect her fiction to be improving, or to bring me information, or to take certain social positions. I do really think that fiction doesn't have to play that role.

Gordimer: I'm not suggesting that it has. I'm simply saying, if we're talking about the phenomenon that it seems possible that you can still have a subject and write the kind of novel that we agree is what literature is about, is what imaginative literature should do. Why is it that so many writers seem not to be able to apply the modernist sensibilities to a subject, or not to be interested? They find subjects, they're not writing without subjects.

Sontag: But could it be something about the way most writers live? They are academics very often in the United States. Most serious writers make a living as teachers, they live in the University world, so now we have a lot of university novels as well as novels about writers. In Europe they might work for television, or be cultural journalists. But that's not an option that's open to Americans, because we have terrible television and we have very little cultural journalism. But isn't it for that reason that writers — perhaps there is a narrowing of subject matter, because their actual field of experience, once they've finished having their childhood, their unhappy marriage, and their first.. their university lives, let's say, and that little bit of capital of experience that they share with everyone of their generation, roughly, to the age of 30, that they have an experience which no longer does open onto the world.

Gordimer: Ah, but did they ever? Did Flaubert? Did Proust? No. And what you're suggesting is indeed a journalistic solution, that they should go out and look for their subjects. They should go then and watch how the miners are reacting to their life during the strike and I don't mean that at all.

Sontag: No. I don't think that writers have to be journalists, but I think that Flaubert and Proust, precisely to take those two writers, had infinitely more experience of society than the average middle-class writer today. I mean, for instance, they knew the upper class of their society. Practically no writers know the upper-class, the real ruling class of their own society. They don't even know where they are. Flaubert was received by the Emperor, and the later part of his life he was a courtier. He was someone who was in the salon of Napoleon III and his sister. Proust we know had a life which brought him into contact with the ruling class of his society. They could write about power, for instance, in a way that contemporary writers can't. They can write about power in the University, or power in a publishing house.

Gordimer: I can't see why contemporary writers can't still write about power. Indeed, it's a subject that interests me very much, and that I often feel I write about

Sontag: Good writers on the whole don't write about where the real sources of social power are. They write about private situations. Because I think in fact they have a narrower social experience — and I'm not talking about becoming journalists.

Living in the Interregnum

Sontag: An American writer whom I know and admire enormously, William Gaddis, once asked me — we were doing a reading together, public reading together — and in the intermission, we were backstage, he said to me 'what emotion do you write out of, Susan?'

That's the kind of question, you know that when you are asked that question it means that the questioner wants to tell you his answer and you're just filling in so that he can get to announce his side of the stories. And I said, without hesitating — and of course it's a preposterous question to narrow down the source of your writing to one emotion — I said, 'grief.' And he said, 'oh, for me it's rage.' And of course, that was what he had wanted to tell me.

I was very struck by my own answer, although his is equally odd. I didn't know that that's what I felt, but I realise that my writing comes out of a deep pessimism and I think that we do live in a time that we all experience in some way as a time of crisis, as a time in which much has been destroyed and much has been lost and much more is going to be lost. And we experience the demand on us as writers, and I think, also, and why not, as human beings, to be both a radical demand and a conservative demand. It's radical because we want to help change what is evil in our society and bring to birth something better, correct, help correct, assist in the correction of certain fundamental wrong and injustices. And we're also conservative because we know that this process, in this process, historical process, so much is being destroyed that we cherish and that we value.

It's very difficult to call ourselves either conservatives, or radicals, because we understand both impulses, just as the labels of Left and Right seem now obsolete. Why should we still be bound to describing ourselves in terms of the seating arrangements for the assembly that met at the time of the French Revolution? And yet, you and I both have identified ourselves with the Left, in so far as we accept these obsolete labels and still would, though perhaps with differing degrees of despair and commitment. And that informs one's situation as a writer, one is part of a process of civilization and one is part of a process of increasing barbarism.

Gordimer: I still believe with Jean Paul Sartre that socialism is the horizon of the World. Of course, I think that we are living in what I have called a state of interregnum. Not only in the country where I come from, South Africa, where it is most marked, because there it's a perfect illustration of Gramsci's statement: the old is dying and the new cannot be born. And in the state of interregnum there arise many morbid symptoms. So I can almost write a novel now, or a story, and call it '*Morbid Symptoms*' and I could just put that as a title almost on anything that I might write.

Sontag: And on a great deal of 20th century literature.

Gordimer: And on a great deal of 20th century literature. I think that it has become more and more a literature of these morbid symptoms. Something is dying, and what we're seeing is that something, the new that we hoped for, doesn't seem to be being born. I think that this is the mental condition of people in the Left, like ourselves!

Sontag: But why do you say that you still think of this as the horizon? Doesn't one need some real examples of societies which are alternatives to the capitalist society? I have heard you say, on many occasions, that you don't believe that capitalism or Western-style democracy can solve the problems of your own country, that there is no evidence that they can solve the problems of your own country. Obviously I could not presume to speak about what the viable future is for your country, but I know that the historical hope in what has called itself socialism has been systematically disappointed by regimes which have started out so promisingly and turned into bureaucratic dictatorships under the domination of an important form of imperialism, Soviet imperialism, or whatever. It seems to me that one has to change the horizon of one's hopes if history does not support them.

Gordimer: But I think has history been given a chance? I would agree with everything that you've said about the experiments one might call them, so far, in various countries. It's really a moment in history. It's not very long, it's a couple, a few generations. Can one, then, on that evidence, accept that the whole idea of socialism, the whole social order, is something that can never be achieved, that there's something inherent?

Sontag: But I certainly think that a more humane society could be achieved. And in that sense, in that very limit — almost tautological sense, I too remain an optimist, or I too have a horizon of hope. But I do not believe that the traditional formulas operate, because we know more about what makes an economy, about what makes a society. The whole situation of modern bureaucracy and the new technologies have altered the way societies are run and the question of how to deal with resources, the internationalisation of all important markets, I think that the economic and the political and historical basis for a great deal of what was the socialist hope, that you could, for example, build socialism in one country — you can't build anything in just one country, because we're all on the Titanic together. We have a world economy which absolutely changes the whole, all the traditional political options, I think.

For a writer, and for a human being who has been inspired by this kind of hope — and I think it's not irrelevant here to talk about writers, because the modern vocation of the writer comes very much out of the horizon of hope that was created first of all by the French Revolution. The earliest writers in the modern sense, precisely do emerge in the time of the French Revolution and the period that prepared for it. That is, the writer who assumes the role of conscience for the society, to report on the society, to be responsible for and to the society. That was an horizon of hope, and if it is true that this 200 year history is in some sense drawing to an end, if we have to at least entertain that possibility in the West, we have to have different goals, different aspirations, which does not mean we simply resign ourselves to the status quo, but we don't continue with this 200 year-old language which has become emptied of sense, then that also must affect the role of the writer and how we conceive of the writer. And there are no images of what the writer does, I think, which we have to pay attention to.

Gordimer: But I think we're both resistant to the idea that the role of the writer should be determined by such things.

Sontag: Well, inevitably we think that the writer has some ethical responsibility. Even those who have seemed to most defend the private vocation of the writer, the responsibility of the writer simply to the language and to the sensibility of the culture, whether you think of Joyce, or again for Virginia Woolf or Nabokov, all turn out to have very important political, social and ethical convictions. That certainly we share. I don't think that the writer is supposed to be a journalist, but that the writer does have some kind of responsibility or accountability.

Gordimer: But if, as a writer, you find yourself living in what I call the state of interregnum, it's marked in my own society, because truly the old order, the old colonial order, which is what apartheid really is — it's the final product of colonialism, it may not have been practised by other colonisers, or it may not have been practised in other forms of colonies before they became independent in different parts of the world, but it is the very last colonial bastion, and it may not be falling, it's decaying from underneath — and living there is living in a state of interregnum, because whatever the new society is going to be, at the moment it's unable to be born. So one's living in this balance.

Now I relate that to the state that you might feel yourself in, in America, but being indeed a writer of the world, somebody who is not particularly tied to any particular country, more attached to a literary culture than to a country. That's more or less how you've defined yourself. But do you too feel because of this, how can I call it, disillusion with the Left, because we didn't think that there was illusion there, there were true possibilities, it seemed that a better society could be achieved through socialist aims, but as you've pointed out, we have seen in 200 years, that's about eight generations, we've seen it fail, mainly, again and again, and particularly now, in our own time. Do you have the sense of being in a spiritual interregnum, but you simply don't know what you can build your sense of continuity on? I mean in a future at all. Can you see a future at all?

Sontag: You see, now I don't know whether your situation is more in advance of mine, historically, or a more retrograde situation. Sometimes, I think your situation is actually a very old-fashioned one.

Gordimer: Oh, I think it is.

Sontag: That is to say, you live in a country where you believe there is a certain inexorable historical process. It cannot be that South Africa will continue to be governed by its white minority. Black rule is inevitable, whether it happens in five years or fifty years, something inevitably is going to change in the society in a direction which you believe is desirable.

Gordimer: Which I believe is right.

Sontag: Yes, in other words, you live in a society characterised by change which you think both desirable and inevitable. This change is going to happen. Whatever its consequences, it is a change that should take place. Whatever the consequences of black rule are, black rule must come. I live in a society and I think it's true largely for people in Western Europe, Britain, North America, at least Canada and the United States, where people no longer have a sense of inexorable and desirable change. They do not believe that certain changes, except possibly changes for the worst, are inevitable. They do not see that they are on the edge of something that they can only assent to or subscribe to. One has rather a defensive feeling towards change. Change is mainly something that destroys the continuity of the generations.

The one thing that we're taught as citizens of a rich consumer society is that the future will not be like the past, that new technologies promise to transform our lives. And we are trained to be consumers of these new technologies, to be consumers in the destruction of our past and our continuity with the past. That has had, I think, enormous and largely negative impact on what personality is, what individuality is, and what all sorts of cultural and intellectual enterprises might be.

If I write, it's because I make an assumption which is thoroughly anacronistic: that the future will somehow be like the past. But most of the information that my society gives me is that it will not be like the past. And I can only view this with dismay. You do not view the change that is coming in your society with dismay.

Gordimer: Well, with apprehension. Because I don't know what kind of change it's going to be. But there is an obstinate belief and a fervent hope, in other words there's still enthusiasm in me. There is still belief that it will be possible to create an alternative Left. I believe that people like us, who have seen the Left betray itself, in many countries, who've seen regimes turning to dictatorships, new forms of imperialism, I still believe that it's possible to create a new Left to move on from there. And I believe, indeed it's an almost apocalyptic feeling, that this has to be done, that we've got to do it.

And vis-à-vis my own country, the difference is, you see, that we're in this political and ideological interregnum. You, to a certain extent are the same as I am, because of this feeling of what has happened to the socialist regimes that we had hopes for, but you believe and you know that there are things worth preserving in the society that you are in, and you'd like to see them carried on. You'd like to see that continuity there. Truly, I have to wrack my brains to think of something that I would like to see preserved in South Africa.

CHAPTER 3

A New Europe

E.P. Thompson and George Konrad

Edward Thompson is one of Britain's most formidable historians and social critics. One of the major figures in the New Left of the fifties, he emerged as the leading spokesman for a pragmatic and humane Marxism. His historical writings influenced both Marxist theory and English social history for a generation. More recently, Thompson has returned to direct political activism in the cause of nuclear disarmament. A prolific essayist, he has criticised the escalating arms race, which he sees as a form of exterminism. In his attacks on both superpowers Thompson has returned consistently to the need to dismantle the iron curtain and free Europe from the divisions imposed at the end of the Second World War.

George Konrad is one of Eastern Europe's most distinguished writers. An internationally acclaimed novelist, he is also a respected political and social commentator. In his latest political essays he has criticised the Yalta agreement of 1945 when Europe was divided by the victors of World War Two. Forty years later he asks whether we can find a realistic political strategy to escape the conflicts between West and East. Emphasising the common interests and culture of both parts of Europe, he calls for a new dialogue across the iron curtain transcending the misunderstanding and clichés of the Cold War, but a genuine dialogue between peoples rather than just states.

Thompson: Welcome to England George, it's great to see you. I remember the first time we met was in Budapest in September 1982. I'd been invited over to talk about the peace movement by a group of young Hungarians, graduate students, some higher form schoolkids, who had formed a new organisation called *Dialogue*, which was dialogue inside Hungary, dialogue between Hungary and the Western peace movement. And my first feeling was how incredible it should be that this beautiful European city and its lively people who were full of enquiry should be thought of as belonging to the other side of the world, across an iron curtain. In a sense, one of the first things for a healing process to try and recover a sense of Europe is to recover it in our own minds. So that increasingly Europeans refuse to accept this and see a flow of culture, flow of ideas and coverging interests. The work we're engaged in is partly an intellectual re-creation of the notion of Europe before the political re-creation can take place. And I remember in 1945, and it's now 40 years that this division has been there, it would have seemed absurd that this division took place. I suppose we were romantic, we were euphoric. We saw in Eastern Europe movements of resistance to fascism which were giving rise to what appeared to be popular front governments. We thought that some of the national communist parties who'd engaged in resistance really in good faith were trying to pursue a popular front policy. But by 1948 that had all collapsed in a mess of foul trials and mendacity, and what is called Yalta, to my mind, in a sense didn't come at the moment of Yalta, it came about 3 years later.

Konrad: Yes, in '45 there was a very special atmosphere in Hungary. I should tell you that when I was a child I listened regularly to the BBC — it was prohibited because Hungary was an ally of Germany — and my father listened to it twice every day. He also listened to Radio Moscow in Hungarian. And it was the hope that these beautiful words about each other — because the BBC always said 'the victorious Red Army' and so on — would be the normal situation of Europe and of this country, and my teacher in the school said 'now we don't teach English but we will teach it after the war.' And that a normal exchange of goods and books and people in Europe would be the natural situation of our life — it was a conviction. Everybody believed it. Yes, then came the new situation. The Russian soldier arrived in Hungary, the Soviet army. I had seen them as liberators and everybody was full of dreams and utopias, and I can tell you that the top of the society — the leaders of the town — disappeared. They went toward the West with the withdrawal of the German and Hungarian troops. But there started a new self-management and self-governing. From out of the ground came a new national committee and everybody began to do something of what he believed to be correct. And there were everywhere parties, in the different clubs of peasants and craftsmen, the different peasants' parties, social democratic parties, there were eight parties. But for me as a child it was very interesting because I visited all these meetings and everybody said something interesting that the others didn't say. So I was really for the pluralism of this country because it was for me a wonderful impression of the flourishing liberty, freedom. And then, you are absolutely right, slowly this diversity and this pluralism disappeared under the pressure of — not only of the communist party and of the political police — but also under the pressure of the presence of the Soviet army.

Thompson: And by remaining there they keep the Americans there. The missiles confront each other. They harden at every stage this division. It's now 40 years. There is no strategy in the great powers, the super-powers, to overcome this. The Warsaw Pact has just been reaffirmed for another 20 years. There's no question of NATO ever being disbanded. So we now have to ask if there is another strategy, and what we've been looking for in the Western peace movement, or very substantial sections of the Western peace movement have been looking for, has been one in which instead of being either for freedom and being confrontational or being for peace and appearing then to be capitulating to the power of the other side, the two movements could recognise each other and find a convergent strategy in which the movements for civil rights in the East would look for natural alliance with peace movements or labour and liberal movements in the West who would then try and find a common policy of a healing process. Now is this utopian? Do you see any way in which this can be done?

Konrad: Yes. I would like to mention that in '55, after the state contract about Austria, we had the hope that somehow we will have the same chance in Hungary. In the next year came the Hungarian revolution, in '56. It was an experiment in how to get out from the blocs unilaterally, from one bloc. It was this declaration of the Hungarian government of Imre Nagy that Hungary wouldn't like to take part in the Warsaw Pact treaty, Hungary would like to be a neutral country in Europe, in the centre of Europe. Three days later came the Soviet intervention and you know the consequences. It was a hard event, I could say. A lot of my fellow compatriots died in this experiment. We had to reflect on it. My friends went away, a lot of my friends went away to the West. Half of my schoolmates left Hungary and those who remained understood that we would remain in this situation, that peace is not so easy, that self determination is not so easy, that peace is very expensive. The dominant reality is the military reality and the military status quo somehow determines the social processes.

Then came another hope in '68 in Czecholovakia, maybe this step-by-step gradual liberalisation and pluralisation of the system will be acceptable to the Soviet Union. No success. Poland, maybe a limited social contract, a free union, an independent union, and one-party system as two partners of the dialogue. This dialogue was cut off by the martial law. So the three main East Central European nations had to understand that first, the Soviet Union doesn't agree with this kind of self-determination, second that the West accepts this fact de facto, third that nobody wants war to change this situation, so these national ways out from this bloc situation aren't very efficient.

Now we are in a very special period in the 'eighties, and we have to understand that armaments and the arms race doesn't come from itself, doesn't come from the development of the weaponry. It comes from this political division of the world and of Europe — from the very fact of the blocs. Therefore we are in a new period of world history, we are living in the period of the bloc system, of the bloc states, and maybe the nation state is only a county in the bloc state and maybe we are living in a period where the real historical political social reality is this bloc state. Then we can ask how can these bloc states decompose themselves?

Thompson: I agree with what you say, but one has to ask 'are we being utopian?' In a sense we are saying that what we need to control are not arms but the armed states. We have to control the states, not to just deal with trying to control arms. And we're also saying that the only realism is utopianism because what Wright Mills used to called the crackpot realism of the military is leading us to a terminus of nuclear war. I mean, the blocs are fixed in this way, that unless one tackles that central problem there is no outcome short of nuclear war. And I think in 20 or 30 years.

This seems to me to be one of the contradictions we're in, that you and I both loathe politics. I mean, you would rather be writing novels, I would rather be writing history, yet we have been forced, because our art and our history is threatened, to become political actors of a kind and to devote a lot of time to thinking and writing about it. And yet the way we're doing it is, I think, correctly described by you as *anti-politics*, in the sense you wish to have a movement of ideas and a healing of cultural relations, a development of people-to-people detente of an active kind, not just passive stabilisation of blocs but an *active* exchange of ideas and people below the blocs, which will go before the political resolution. So that the utopians have got to start to heal the blocs before the politicians will do anything about it.

Konrad: Yes, I agree that it is at the terminal stage that the politicians are at the summit table and they kiss each other, as Khrushchev and Kennedy did. But it has to be prepared. And my thesis is, and as I see your whole activity in the last years, that we intellectuals are the initiators. And why we are motivated to do it is because we are disturbed by the politics. Personally I mentioned this '44, this year, then it was a dangerous year, it was as if politics would somehow kill me, in a very direct form. Then I had some troubles — problems as a bourgeois.

Thompson: I'm sorry, I don't quite understand you.

Konrad: Yes, in Hungary I was a class enemy. I was not a class enemy in myself but I was treated so.

Thompson: In which year was this?

Konrad: It was in the 'fifties, the Stanlinist period, you know? I was thrown out from the university. Professor George Lukacs helped me back. It was an interesting period, I learned a lot. But then came '56, it was however a strong determination of my situation to be there. And I had the feeling that in this part of Europe intellectuals feel that their own fate, their individual everyday life is somehow related to the politics so they can't avoid it. And those who seem to be apolitical are very clever politicals because they know very exactly what not to touch, what to avoid — about what they should not speak.

But it seems to me that in the 'eighties the Western European intellectuals have arrived also at this image of their own life, that they are dependent, and they are even threatened and war can put in flames your whole life from one moment to the other. So now we are both in a quite disagreeable situation. It would be a little bit arrogant if I would say that we were the first runners in this understanding. But this comprehension is now a little bit mutual. As also the moves are mutual.

Thompson: But it's easy to say that the intellectual should be a communicator, should build bridges that others can go over, should refuse..

Konrad: But are the politicians a very special zoological race?

Thompson: Ah, I wasn't thinking so much of the politicians, I was asking if intellectuals say they have a special role are they in fact asking for special privileges? Is this an elitist attitude? If intellectuals say 'we refuse the growing pressures of the security state. We are not the citizens of blocs. We are not citizens of NATO or the Warsaw Pact, we belong to Europe...'

Konrad: We create Europe with this activity. Europe is not the Europe of the state. Europe is the culture of the real existing relationships. Europe is here in our conversation.

Thompson: This is not just for people who are in distinct organisations or peace movement people with badges. This is work for all communicators, and not only for professional intellectuals, but people in churches, in societies and trade unions should be all the time directing their activity to trying to make these bridges.

Konrad: Of course the East European people who travel to Paris or London or Vienna realise that we belong to the same culture. Or not only we belong, we *want* to belong to it, because we also have had cultural relationships for thousands of years. The Gothic cathedrals are here in Canterbury and in my country, they're in Budapest, in Rumania, in Transylvania. It's a philosophical change, I'm sure, which is the most important. The philosophical change which is somehow related to the end of this euphoria of industrialisation, that we understand better the importance of history. We understand better that our reality is not the reality of the generals, of the marshals. We can't let ourselves be identified with the politics of the political classes. It is the anti-politics that we have our own life and we don't want to be dependent on them, and we aren't dependent on them in the very ways in which we describe, how we understand, how we interpret our world. And I can say that they are not the initiators of the culture. What they have in their brain is somehow an input. And they are not so autonomous in their ideologies. Without intellectuals the bloc system and the cold war is not possible.

Thompson: Without tame intellectuals?

Konrad: Yes.

Thompson: But there is a difficulty in what you're saying, which is that the culture you speak of is a particular historical vision of European culture. And there are a lot of voices now that are watching us critically that say aren't the aspirations of the European peace movement, the aspirations of *Charter 77* or the democratic opposition, or even the aspirations of *Solidarnosc*, because the Polish movement has been very much locked into its own Polish perspectives, aren't these Eurocentric? They would also argue, I think perhaps Noam Chomsky would argue, that the true, real economic and strategic roots of the Cold War lie in the Third World, that the contest of the two superpowers for dominance and also for resources in the Third World, that this is where in fact the pain of the Cold War is felt most and if we are asking to heal the continent of Europe as advanced nations, we are failing in our responsibilities to the Third World? Now I don't agree with this, but I can understand that when we're sitting here talking about re-healing, healing Europe once again, that it might seem to a Third World person that..

Konrad: You have also to think of the fact that now it is the 30th anniversary of the Bandung priciples. And this was the principle of the Non-Aligned world. And the Third World was the part of this world which didn't fall into this bloc division, bloc confrontation. Most of these Third World countries tried to keep themselves outside of this bloc confrontation. So not only has the Third World to learn from Europe but Europe also has to learn from the Third World.

Thompson: I've just come back from China and I wouldn't pretend to understand China, but the language increasingly being used is against precisely the bi-polar division of the world. They were very active at the 30th anniversary of Bandung and the language I heard there, if it is truly the direction they're moving in, is back into a much more non-aligned position in which they see their natural allies as being a non-aligned movement in Europe. They don't resent what we're doing at all. China may be a special case. However, I think probably we have to always interpret and explain what we're doing to the Third World because this is a movement of ideas which seems somehow exclusive if we talk about it only in European terms.

Konrad: But is it not possible that we have very different levels of consciousness? So we have a national level, and I would like to dramatise the importance of national identities in this period of the bloc confrontation because these national identities, these new nationalisms — and we are in the 'eighties in a period of new nationalisms — means that people want to have a polycentric world. That this bi-polar world is not the true expression of the world's social reality, because why should not Budapest also be a pole and why not London and Copenhagen also? So maybe every nation is a pole of this world. And if we accept this idea then we can go further, we can say that towns and movements and individuals and persons, and we arrive at the intellectuals, are also poles. So if we have the utopia of a polycentric world instead of a morbid utopia of a bi-polar world, if we have a philosophy of real pluralism instead of this mortal dualism, then maybe we arrive to the point of the decomposition of the blocs. And then we arrive also at the problem that we have local patriotic identities and feelings and knowledge, but we have also some European, some central European regions, and some world consciousness in this period of the media. We arrive at some solidarity with other continents. So I don't believe that they exclude each other.

Thompson: This pluralism might be taken a stage further, in the sense of a little bit more pluralism of categories, because in our heads there's still this very powerful tendency to sort nations into 'capitalists' and 'socialists' as if they were absolutely distinct and completely categorically divided from each other. And so you get, I find, in the West — and certainly I find minds in the East trapped by the notion that 'well, in the end the blocs are radically and totally different kinds of social system, economic and social system, and to talk of a healing process is completely ignoring the fact that capitalism is capitalism, socialism is socialism.' Even if you say it's corrupted socialism or it's primitive socialism that's got to learn new ways, you still say they can never get across this division.

I noticed you said in *Anti-politics* something about post-capitalist and post-communist societies. I said something very much the same in one of my essays in *The Heavy Dancers*, that we become lost in these categories and that we may be approaching a time in which they are decomposing and we have to find new names and new definitions. And whether we might not be coming to a time, for example, when the entire history of the social democratic international and the communist international as being absolutely opposed to each other is seen as a past historical phase. So that the economic diversification which is going on in Hungary and, incidentally, in a rather different way, in China also, may be showing that there are different shades and adaptations and there's no reason why social democratic West Germany can't exist as a system perfectly well with a more diversified Hungary with a more diversified market economy.

Konrad: I wouldn't say that Hungary can be described by this notion 'socialism', 'state socialism', 'corrupted socialism', 'developed socialism' and so on. It is a period of this country and it is also so in Poland or Czechoslovakia, or even in the Soviet Union, that nations have centuries and centuries and we have now spent 40 years in this period when we spoke a lot about socialism. We have very different institutions and books in the bookshops and in the homes and ideas in our heads and it's impossible to reduce this variety of phenomena and ideas to this one notion 'socialism'. It would be an imperialism of the theoreticians.

Thompson: Well, your imperialism, George, is to propose as a general case, as a general advocacy, anti-politics. And in this it seems to me you're saying that now in the — well, at any time really after World War Two if not before, the problem of the century has become the state, the problem of the century becomes the state and above all the armed state now, and that one does not continue with what you call Jacobin-Leninist attempts to overthrow the state and establish a counter-state. One doesn't contest, to try and replace those in power with other people in power, one tries to decompose power. And this is a task which really does give a great deal of identity, common identity, to the Western peace movement which is trying to decompose its own power structures and which can feel the security state growing, and to the movement to democratise and bring rights, trade union and civil rights in Eastern Europe. Both are movements trying to limit the power of the state, to enlarge the area of civil society and, as you say, to establish a counter-power of opinion and of free individual association and of the formation of ideas which the state can't stop and it can't penetrate.

Konrad: Yes. Maybe the nation state as an expression of nationalism is, in this very strong integrational period of itself, of its own society, a transitory phenomenon. So maybe there are tendencies under the state and above the state in the low world of human communication, and above the state — I would like to say 'under the state' means local communities, self-government, self-management of factories, of working groups, of very different informal face-to-face organisations — and there is this world-wide integration of markets, of industry, and of communications and post and transport, and then maybe we can push the nation state into its own place. It was too fat. It should be a little bit more svelt. And maybe this anti-political attitude or point of view is only a tendency not to overthrow, not to demolish the state, not to make

an armed revolt against it, but to make a political culture in which
the state returns to its proper place. It has a lot to do. It has very
much to do and when it would like to do everything then it's maybe
doing nothing. When the state is overcharged then the state is
powerless. When the state determines everything in the economy
then the economy will be very ill. So this anti-political mentality
means that the civil society has its own civil courage to tell the fellow
politicians 'my friend you should do your own work and don't you
confiscate my manuscript.'

Thompson: I wonder if I could become an interviewer for a
moment? The manner in Britain is to be rude and abrasive if you are
an interviewer, but I ask you how far you are generalising from
exceptional Hungarian experience? Would a Pole or a Czech say
'well, George Konrad can say this because he comes from a very
special case in Hungary?' How far is it a special case? I don't know,
I think some western visitors, because your ruling party is much
more civilised and more flexible and more courteous than, for
example, in Czechoslovakia or the GDR which is still a Prussian
communist state, they think it's a really lovely nice perfect place,
Hungary, and don't understand both the pain and the suffering
which people who try for autonomy have to endure and they don't
also always understand the limits upon what is permissible in
Hungary. I noticed this when I was there and I am no expert. And
the word 'provocation' kept on being used. You could not say
certain things because they were a 'provocation.' A great majority
of your people know that they would not like to have Soviet troops
in the country but it is provocative to raise the question. So what I'm
really throwing at you is in generalising from the way Hungarians
have successfully limited and civilised the communists aren't you
taking an exceptional case?

Konrad: Yes. I believe it also. Maybe we were the first in this
self-liberating movement, in this effort at emancipation. It was a
very sincere and dramatic expression of the society in '56, and it was
an expressionist revolution, the society expressed what they really
wanted. In every factory, in every enterprise, in communities, there
were long petitions and visions about the good society, about the
good constitution and so on. So it was a very interesting period and
then came the repression and the Hungarians learned after a certain
apathetic period to work out a *modus vivendi* to live together with
this model which was somehow imposed on them. For example, it is
an illegal conversation we are having now, but, however, it exists,
we made it. So I believe that the regime can't decide about
everything and the society can't liberate itself completely. Now we
are living in a sort of monarchy. It's not a totalitarian regime, it's
maybe an autocratic regime. There are many words for it, but it's

maybe a paternalistic regime, but monarchy can have also fine style at the end and the question is...

Thompson: You mean you would like the communist party to become like the British queen, the British monarchy?

Konrad: Yes, it would be wonderful. And the question is if this little model will be contagious or not. There are some little hopes that maybe it will go through, because if people would like to achieve a certain kind of intensive economics, to consume more, to have peace, to have their own privacy, finally these are embourgoisements. And therefore I believe that there are many ways, even in eastern Europe — you were in Bulgaria, it's a very different kind of model, but if you go from Bulgaria to Hungary then you go through Yugoslavia, how many nations, how many different tendencies? If we accept the very fact that these are also social experiments and if there isn't any war, and if it becomes clearer and clearer that this military status quo of Europe is a surface, and reality is the life of the polycentric nations, then we will arrive in another cultural period which will be post-communist and maybe post-capitalist because then this post-industrial, Green, ecological — I don't know how to describe this new image of the world — will also have results here in the Western world.

Thompson: I'd like to agree with you that this pluralism, this gentle gradient back to a reunited, diverse Europe is in the course of happening, but I wonder if we're not becoming a bit too comfortable? I mean, I want to restate the view of the Western peace movement that the weapons do matter. They are the most ugly symbols, even if they're not used — and they could be used — but they are the most ugly symbols of human relationship that have ever existed. If you are multiplying the means to exterminate your neighbours, you are also reinforcing at every moment the worst tendencies in both blocs. And our perception is that the refusal of nuclear weapons must be absolute. Yes, the ascent to democracy also has to be absolute but both of these must be absolute. If we can demystify the nuclear armoury, if we can actually effectively block or stop some part of it, this itself might generate responses and make more possible the opening of both halves of Europe. Now I know this is sometimes viewed critically on your side of the world, that our absolute position on this — because we do indeed take it seriously, I think that Star Wars itself is one of the most dangerous fantasies of the greatest power in the world, instead of reducing nuclear weapons to carry this entire machinery of technology into space, that could possibly arise and I think it's a delusion which suggests that the powers of militarism are quite beyond human control — so that our absolute position on this is one which sometimes seems over on your side to be either naive or else even to be submissive to the power on your side.

Konrad: It's a terribly difficult problem. We agree with you and with the Western peace movement that the nuclear winter is the final evil, the final solution of the whole human kind, as it was the final solution of the Jews, Auschwitz. So we can say also that the nuclear holocaust is the worst imaginable case of human development and we really are in a period when it is possible. I would like to add that I have seen some posters in West Berlin. On the poster was 'for a nuclear free Europe' and on the other side the slogan was 'for a bloc free Europe.' I think that there is no nuclear free Europe without a bloc free Europe. The denuclearisation of the world is impossible without the decomposition of the blocs, so nobody can avoid the political side of the question. I believe that we need some common ideas and there will be a period when we will share a common platform about the peace order of Europe and if the dissidents of both parts will agree in a peace constitution, in a democratic peace constitution of this continent and maybe of the world, then these misunderstandings between two grassroot move-ments, or between individuals and people who don't belong to any movement, who aren't politicians, will be much better. Maybe we aren't there yet in this wedding period of the movement, but we are on the way and I am sure that one of the most important tasks of the Western peace movement is to *learn*. To learn about themselves, about European political structures, and also about Eastern Europe or about the Soviet Union. But I could tell you that in my country it would be impossible to make a demonstration against the Soviet deployments there. Warheads aren't there, missiles I don't know, maybe, nobody knows and the fact that these military apparatuses are such hidden, sacred, mystical realities, and that we can't control them, not at all, that a Greenham Common revolt would be absolutely impossible in my country, means that we have to have another image about a possible peace movement, because this peace movement you supported and you were pleased to see in '82 was in the next year eliminated by police harassments.

Thompson: In very subtle forms, yes.

Konrad: Very subtle forms, but for a student the possibility that he will be excluded from the university and that he can't continue his studies does however have a danger and a risk — it will break his career. The same possibilities aren't here, in this part of the peace movement, so we are now in the situation that there is no independent peace movement in my country. The people are there, they are doing many other things, maybe they are environmentalists, maybe they do new cultural forms, but the ideas are however there and the thinking is there and maybe there will be a new independent peace movement.

Thompson: I think the peace culture is a culture and not to be identified just with movements and people who wear badges only. I think this is true, and because the identical forms of movement are not possible in the East this doesn't stop us continuing our forms in the West because we have to turn our backs upon power in whatever way is possible. And it's my conviction as an optimist here that the kind of opening which Hungarian *Dialogue* showed and which the *Swords into Ploughshares* in East Germany showed, will return, that this is in the course of history that this is something that will be reborn from the culture, and that our task is to work both against the weapons and against the blocs as part of a common united movement.

Konrad: I hope the young people will do it, and I hope that we will see it.

Thompson: Yes.

CHAPTER 4

Writing for A Future

Günter Grass and Salman Rushdie

Günter Grass is one of West Germany's most distinghished writers. He came to prominence in the early 'sixties with novels which attempted to confront the experience of nazism, straining to find the form adequate to describe Germany's recent past. The result was the so-called *rubble literature* trying to rebuild the German language from the rubble of nazism through an unconventional kind of writing which mixes autobiography and fiction, history and literature. A committed Social Democrat, Grass has always affirmed the political and historical responsibility of the artist. In his later writing this has led him to discuss more pressing contemporary concerns: peace, ecology and divisions in the modern world.

Salman Rushdie is best known as the author of *Midnight's Children* and *Shame*. Highly acclaimed as a novelist, he combines a modernist's sensibility with historical subjects on a grand scale: Indian independence and dictatorship in Pakistan. In both books fiction and fantasy mix together with politics and history. This sense of political responsibility extends to articles in which Rushdie has criticised the British nostalgia for Empire as a failure to come to terms with being a post colonial multi-racial society. Like Grass, he sees the writer as figure of doubt, attacking false certainties in the culture.

To Lose a War

Rushdie: I was thinking about the war and what it was like for the losers as opposed to the winners. And I wondered if you felt that coming from the losing side, so to speak, has disadvantages or has had advantages for you in writing.

Grass: You see, if you accept that you are a loser — and for German people it was very hard to accept — looking back, I think I did win something by this acceptance. By losing the war I lost my hometown, Danzig, that's now Gdansk, that's Polish. And I tried to bring something back to write about, to win it again by writing. I think also it is a chance, if you lose a war, to go on thinking about the reasons why it could happen in Germany, this terrible crime with a short name: Auschwitz. And when I'm visiting other countries who still believe they belong to the winner's side I am very often astonished how less able they are to think about things they have lost.

Rushdie: You see, I was interested in what you said about losing the city, because I had exactly the same sense — for different reasons. It was a simpler reason: my family migrated away from the city. When I was 14 I left to go to school in England. And then the city itself was transformed, because the city that I remember, the city that I grew up in — Bombay — was knocked down and was replaced by high rise buildings, like concrete tombstones. So in a way, even the people who still live in the city lost it because it disappeared. And I very much had the desire of wanting to reclaim it. And it was very useful for me that the city itself was built on land reclamation. The whole city where it now stands, most of it is built on land that was reclaimed from the sea. By the British in fact. Bombay is in a way a British invention as a city. And I felt I had to go through a similar process of land reclamation to get the city back for myself.

Grass: Reading your book I had the feeling that it was somebody trying to reconstruct something for himself writing this book, something he has lost, and to keep it.

Rushdie: That's right. I had the feeling, living in England, you know, that there was that part of my life that was in danger of being lost, was slipping away, and I had to do something before it was too late.

Grass: But it's necessary for writing, perhaps also for other things, to lose something to really love it afterwards.

Rushdie: In order to have something to find.

Grass: To find, yes.

Rushdie: The question of loss is also a question connected to memory, and I find it interesting that a number of leading writers in contemporary European literature approach this subject of reclamation, of regaining the past, of remaking the past, reinventing it for their own purposes. That's to say there is, it seems, all over Europe, a kind of historical project amongst many writers. Well, a historical or a remembering project, the two not being quite the same thing. For instance, I never studied literature, I studied history, and so in my mind that kind of historical approach to the world was in a way natural. And I wondered if for you it had also been something that you consciously had as a subject, the remaking of history, when you started to write.

Grass: Well I started as a young boy. My only wish and my only thinking was to be an artist. I started as a sculptor after the war, a stonemason first, in the cemetery. But at this time I also wrote my first poems, very artistically. And by the middle of the 'fifties I discovered for myself that I did need a confrontation with history, with German history. I couldn't look away any more to other parts, nice parts. It had to be confronted. It was also the reason I moved to Berlin, because here in West Berlin, you are confronted every day with the result of the last war. Even without seeing the wall every day you have this feeling.

Another reason was that just after the war the Germans in both parts tried to belong to the winner's side. We were the best democrats afterwards and we did everything the United States wanted. And you can say the same of East Germany, they were the best socialists and did exactly what Moscow was wanting at this time. And the official language, political language about the end of the war was not of capitulation, it was *disaster*, it was a *catastrophe*, it was *hour zero*. Nice lies, covering the truth. And about the nazi time, they said it was a time when it 'became dark in Germany'. And this kind of demonisation of the SS, of the nazi party, didn't tell the truth. This was one reason to look back and to show in telling my story that all these things happened in broad daylight, very slowly. There were special groups who were interested: Capital, the arrangement between Capital and Hitler in the beginning, but also the petit bourgeois people who were lost after the First World War. It was very easy for Hitler to win those people. He really did speak out the dreams of the petit bourgeois, and in a terrible way he realised what he promised to them. I tried both in my first novel, *The Tin Drum*, but also in *Dog Years*, not to explain, to tell the story of this slow, very petit bourgeois way to go slowly with full knowledge into crime: political crime.

Rushdie: What you're saying is that the purpose of the fiction was in a way paradoxical, that the fiction is telling the truth at a time at which the people who claimed to be telling the truth are making things up. So in a way you have politicians or the media or whoever, the people who form opinion, in fact making the fictions. And it becomes the duty of the writer of fiction to start telling the truth. This is a kind of paradox which perhaps is true of many countries now.

Grass: What do we understand by reality? I think that our dreams and the unspoken things and the fantastic ideas people have all belong to reality. And in one sentence I jump from the flat reality you see, you can touch, to inside things. And then that sentence, the long sentence I like to do, comes back to the flat reality, but changed now. Changed by fantasy. With another accent. And this way of telling a story everybody thought they knew before was surprising for people. Also it was a shock that I put away all this demonisation of the nazi time, that everybody could rediscover himself in this terrible time.

Writing for a Future

Rushdie: it seems to me there are two bodies of thought at the moment which would hold that this is none of our business as writers. There is, certainly inside English literature, but I suspect in all literatures, an attitude towards writing which says that it is somehow separate from these public issues and ought to be separated from them. And on the other hand you have the whole apparatus of the post-modernist critique, which also, for very different reasons, seeks to separate the text from the world. So you have, let's say, both a radical and a conservative discourse suggesting that writers should not meddle in public affairs. I mean, my own inability to believe that that's the case is very strong. And I think it's largely because the first writer I ever met when I was a child as a friend of my family, is a very good Urdu language poet called Faez, who's just sadly died. He was a completely committed political figure — of a different character to myself, because he was a winner of the Lenin Prize, he was a communist poet and remained so all his life — but from him, just by watching him as I grew up, it seemed to me obvious that what a writer should do is also to deal in politics. And it still remains very surprising to me when people say that that's not actually a writer's job, that writers should, you know, tell stories and make things up and not talk about things like that. Now clearly, in your own work you've taken the public road, both inside the novels and in your statements and writings outside the novels. Was that why you became a writer do you think, or did it come as a secondary impulse, that desire to take issue with the affairs of the time?

Grass: No. For me, every problem I see I see as an artist. Also in writing. But the reality I'm crowded around with is touched by politics and if sometimes I wish to write or to do something that has nothing to do with politics, in the second sentence the history of my country, my own history, takes me back to this ugly reality we are living in. When I was a young writer I admired Döblin, I admired Brecht, Thomas Mann and Heinrich Mann and these were all four kicked out from Germany. They had to emigrate. All their life was touched by this problem. Also, when Brecht did come back to Germany and lived in East Berlin, he was confronted with politics. In that year was the first uprising of the workers in Germany, in '53 when he was director of a theatre. I think it's a stupid question. And they always try also in Germany to say 'writer, go write, please, nice things or sad things and poetical things.' As long as we've had literature it was confronted by political questions. And what is moving me in recent years more and more is that the situation of writing has changed, because the situation of life has changed. Human beings for the first time are able to destroy themselves.

After Hiroshima the situation from year to year has changed. We are able, from one day to another, to finish humanity, to end history. This kills our belief that if we are dead our books go on and if people don't understand today they will understand in 50 years, as writers in all centuries could trust to the strongness of time. Time was on the side of the writers. They could say 'you dictator, you Pope, you will be dead, but my book in 100 years and 200 years will still be there.' All the European process of Enlightenment, you can't think about it without this hope. The books were forbidden but they did work. They worked because time was on the side of literature.

Rushdie: Yes, the future existed.

Grass: And this we don't have any more. We cannot be sure about this. I think it was one of the reasons I stopped writing for three years, thinking about this problem. Because it changes the context of it. I want to go on writing, but with this knowledge, and this is a an existential question but also a political question.

Rushdie: Although I know that theoretically, I find it very difficult to believe in fact that there will not be a posterity. I mean, there's a kind of an irrational determination to assume posterity. That's to say that it's very difficult for me to think how my actual writing would be affected by what I know theoretically to be true. I mean, how does one write differently if you cancel the idea of posterity? What does that do to the writing? Anything? I mean, apart from the consciousness of it? Did you find it changed your writing?

Grass: In the book I just wrote I hope I am able to express what has changed. And sure, if I express things like we spoke about, it will also change the form of writing. I can't describe it just now. But if you live here in the middle of Europe, in Germany, and you know that just here the nuclear weapons are crowded from East and West more than in any other part of the world, you must be a lucky man and a bit of a stupid man if you don't realise this — lucky and stupid in the same moment not to realise this every day. And, sure, it's very difficult to go on and live like this, but we have in Germany a lot of young people who are afraid, and they are brave enough to show that they are afraid. I'm afraid of people who still go on and say 'well, there is no reason to be afraid and life will go on and we have to trust'. I think that one of the mistakes the Germans made in this century was that they were not brave enough to be afraid, to show it. This we have to learn. And perhaps, knowing this, we could learn that we are not alone here. There are animals, there is nature. We have to find another connection to nature. I think we have, with all this knowledge we have, we have to go on to tell stories. But with this knowledge.

To Tell a Story

Rushdie: Is it a question of telling stories then? Because it seems to me that the reason, the thing that made me become a writer was that desire, the desire simply to tell stories. I grew up in a literary tradition. By and large the stories I was told as a child were *Arabian Nights* kind of stories. I mean, those sorts of fairy tales. But beyond that, the kind of context in which I began to think was one in which it was accepted that stories should be untrue. You know, the idea that fiction should be a lie, that it should be a wonderful story. That horses should fly, and also carpets, was expected. And the belief that by telling stories in that way, in a marvellous way, you could actually tell a kind of truth which you couldn't tell in other ways. So I grew up assuming that that was the normal way of telling stories and found myself, when I began to write seriously, in the context of a literature which had for a long time formed an opposite view about what a novel was. That's to say, a novel should be mimetic, it should imitate the world, the rules of naturalism or of social realism. So I find myself constantly struggling with the fact that my assumptions are opposite to the assumptions of many people in the West, for whom fantasy or the use of the imagination is exceptional, is unusual. For me it seems to be normative. And I wondered what was the kind of literary context that you came from, whether you had a similar experience or not.

Grass: Just after the war I really started to read again and was interested in all the forbidden literature, like the early expressionism in Germany, the surrealistic authors. For me realism was . . I couldn't work with this short-minded kind of realism just to imitate reality. I was also from my childhood very much touched by this German romantic tradition, the fairy tales. They are telling truth. The flying horse is really flying.

Rushdie: The fish talks.

Grass: Yes, he talks. And I used in many books these archetypical figures of German fairy tales. Like in *The Flounder* and also in *The Tin Drum*. And I think to use these fairy tales is bringing us to another kind of truth. To a much richer truth than you can get by collecting the facts of this flat realism.

Rushdie: Yes, you see, it struck me when I was beginning *Midnight's Children*, particularly, it struck me that here I am trying to describe everyday reality as it's experienced by people who are not Western people and who, to give only the most obvious example, are by and large very religious. I mean, these are people who *actually* believe in God, not in a kind of theoretical symbolised way, but in the actual everyday interpenetration of the divine and the ordinary and the mundane. So it seemed to me that realism, the techniques, the conventions of realism, were completely

inappropriate to describe reality perceived in that way. Because this
is a very rationalistic kind of writing, and so, in a way, the form and
the language would become like a judgement about the people you
were talking about. And so it seemed to me that you have to find a
different way in order to allow that reality to have stature, to exist in
a way in which it's not prejudged. So it seemed that, in a way,
realism was not realistic. That it was a way of falsifying reality rather
than expressing it. And I feel that more and more really. That this is
a narrow convention that somehow has become canonical, has
become the thing that is called reality, whereas in fact it's just
another game.

Grass: I use reality, when I speak in the German language, in the
plural. We have many realities. And the second sort is a political
one because our problem is that we don't accept that there are many
realities. One side wants only this reality, and the other only their
own reality. And this is one of the reasons we still have this this
struggle. There is one chapter in *The Flounder*, the title of the
chapter is 'The Other Truth', going back to the Grimm brothers.

Rushdie: Oh yes, with the mushrooms.

Grass: Yes, they are collecting fairy tales, and one German
painter of the romantic period, Runge, did write down some
marvellous fairy tales in low German. And he is recounting the
story that this old woman had told him, the fairy tale of the
fisherman and his wife. They tell him two versions. In one version
the wife always wants more and more and to become the King and
the Pope and, in the end, God. And then both were punished and
that's the end. And the other version is that the man always wants
more and more. And there's a struggle between what truth they will
use.

Rushdie: And they settle on the woman?

Grass: And they settle on the woman, yes. And Runge said it was
our problem, that we are not able to accept that there are two
possibilities of truth. We always want one, one reality.

Rushdie: In India the thing that I've taken most from, I think,
apart from the fairy tale tradition that we were talking about, is the
oral narration. Because it is a country of still largely illiterate people
and so the power and the vitality still remains in the oral story-
telling tradition. And what's interesting about these stories is that
they command huge audiences, the best story tellers, with literally
hundreds of thousands of people. They'll come to sit in a field while
a man tells stories. It's a very eclectic form, and of course is not at all
linear. I mean, the story does not go from the beginning to the end
but it goes in these great loops and circles back on itself, repeats
earlier things, digresses, uses sometimes a kind of Chinese box
system, where you have the story inside the story inside the story

and then they all come back. And it seems to be formlessness. When you look at it it appears to be chaos, that simply that you are at the whim of the story teller and he can do whatever he wants.

Now, it occurred to me to ask the opposite question. Let us assume, for the sake of argument, that this is not formlessness but that this is a form which after all is many thousands of years old and has adopted this shape for good reasons. Now, if so, what would those reasons be? And it struck me the answer is very simple, which is that the story teller, much more so than the novelist, has the problem of holding the audience, and that the novelist doesn't see the moment at which people shut the book and get bored. The story teller always sees the moment because they get up and walk away, or they throw eggs or whatever. So everything he does is done to hold the audience. And suddenly this suggested to me that what we were being told was that this very gymnastic form, this very convoluted, complicated form was in fact the reason why people were listening. That it was actually more interesting to listen in that way than it was to listen to a story which went from the beginning to the middle to the end. And this was, it struck me, a sort of reversal of a conventional wisdom about form, which is that if a form is complicated it puts people off. Here was the proof, these hundreds of thousands of people were the proof that the acrobatics in the form were actually what was keeping them sitting there, hooked. You know, it was just like a juggler throwing six balls into the air, and of course the audience is waiting for him to drop them. And the fact that he doesn't drop them is why you go on watching. And just when you think he can't possibly do it any more, he throws three more balls up and then he's juggling nine balls. And it's that kind of skill, that pyrotechnics, that I tried to say 'all right, now we can also do that in literature, we don't have to go from the beginning to the middle to the end. We can use this kind of game.' And then I found, in novels like *Tristram Shandy*, for example, a very similar spirit. A very similar spirit. So it seemed to me that what I was finding out was the kind of writing that stood, so to speak, at the frontier between both the cultures. That I could, as a migrant from that culture into this culture, that I could bring with me that luggage and already find that there was a similar thing going on. So I had something to connect myself to.

Grass: It's interesting what you said about the story teller, that his story is like a chaos. What I tried in recent years more than in the first books was to use the form of the essay as a told story. To bring it into the told story as a part of this chaos.

Rushdie: Yes. Also you enter the books more now. I mean, there is a figure, more and more a figure which the book asks us to identify as the author inside the text.

Grass: Yes, but this changes. The author is writing the book and I don't look any more for another figure to hide myself behind. Because I trust much more my own possibility to jump into the book to tell the story and to be changed by the fiction. I come out as another person afterwards when I finish the book. The critics, they like to to search, to make a search for the author in the main character. And I think the author is in all the figures, also in the little ones. He has to be, he has to be inside in all the figures. If he is not they're not alive and they can't exist. And you know also when you start a book after some 50, 100 pages the figures are there and then they act as they want.

Rushdie: Yes and they change it.

Grass: It happened very often to me that I tried to make some experience for them and force them to do this and they didn't want to. I really had these kinds of reactions, I had these kinds of discussions. I made dirty tricks.

Rushdie: To make them do things.

Grass: Yes. Perhaps during writing *The Tin Drum* my plan was to give Oskar Mazerath a sister. He just didn't want her. He didn't want her. I couldn't go on writing because he didn't want a sister. And this is one of the reasons, because I saw this kind of sister figure, that I made this figure then in *Cat and Mouse* and *Dog Years* in Tula Pokriefke. I understood him after a while. It couldn't work, these two people together, Tula Pokriefka and Oskar Mazerath would have been too much. They would have killed each other.

Rushdie: This is very interesting because I also have this in *Shame*, the most recent novel. There's a dictator, a General in a country like Pakistan and he falls and in the novel as it exists he's killed. I mean he dies. Now originally I didn't think it would be necessary for him to die. I wanted him to fall but I thought maybe he could go into exile. And when he falls and he's fleeing towards the frontier — and the novel makes much of the idea of the frontier, because what it says is that in a dictatorship the frontier is like a trap, it's a thing that you can't pass, and in the novel people tend to faint when they come to a frontier, the frontier is equated with the edge of the world — so the point is that the character had understood this better than the author, so that when the General reached the frontier he simply informed me that he couldn't cross. It was not possible for him to. And I made many attempts to bully him across the frontier and he wouldn't go. So in the end I was forced to accept that he has to stay here, and if he was forced to stay inside the country then there was no possibility that he could be left alive, so then he had to be killed. So he committed suicide in a way. I was arranging an old age for him in England but he decided to stay at home.

Grass: I am just writing another book now. I have the strange experience of speaking again and working again with Oskar Mazerath 30 years later. Now he is 60 years old and I get the same strange reactions when I try to do something with him he doesn't want. I tried to kill him. And he is very resistant.

A Sense of Place

Rushdie: Of course in my situation I do get asked, and indeed I ask myself, quite a lot about the idea of a place, about where I am to put the sense of home. Certainly, for instance, when I go to Bombay still I always have a kind of emotion on arriving that other places don't give me, in a way that is a sense of home. But also my family are in Pakistan and my own life is in England and all these places have claims on me. And so sometimes I answer the question by saying that it's not as if I've been uprooted so much as if I have too many roots. It's a kind of excess. A surfeit of roots, which are planted in all these different places. And then at other times it doesn't feel like that and it feels more like that the only place that I can really find the sense of home is, so to speak, inside language. That when I'm inhabiting the language is where I actually feel more myself than at other times. So, as it were, the act of writing becomes home.

Grass: I have this feeling of arriving also when I go back to Gdansk and I see the city as it is rebuilt by Polish people now, but after some minutes I know it is no longer Danzig and I know that it's lost. And I accept it is. And to be now without a place, to be with many places, I think it's a very good feeling to be without one place, to be nervous, to be disturbed, to be out, to belong to the loser and to know what you have lost. And to carry it in language. And now, coming to the point you ask me, sure, language can be something like home for a writer, but I think I would have this feeling and this relation to language also if I had a place, and I think the same would happen to you. But we Germans have this special problem that this is a reason for our neighbours to be nervous again. For other people it's very simple, young people, to explain themselves as English or Dutch or French or Spanish. But it's much more difficult for young people in Germany. They have to explain that they're from West Germany or from East Germany. We are afraid to use a word like nation. If somebody in Germany speaks quite normally about the German nation everybody is afraid there's a new nationalism coming. It's a kind of taboo. And one of the reasons that we don't find a way to live as German people in two states as neighbours is we all expected that the winners of the war would give us a chance to come together. But there is no reason in Poland or France to help the Germans to come together. After the experience of two world wars in the middle of Europe there are reasons to think it's quite good that they are divided. But this cannot be the end of the story. If we don't find a way there will be a vacuum. We can't avoid the national question. And if we don't give answers to the young generations, there can be a danger that they need for themselves this feeling of belonging to a nation, and the danger of a new kind of nationalism. And this is one of the reasons I say to my leftwing friends we now have to take care of these questions. We always got wrong answers to the question of nation from the Right side, from Bismark up to Hitler, and we cannot ignore this question. We have now to try to give an answer from our experience, our point of view. This leads me from the language to the much, much more important question for German people.

Rushdie: Ah, you see, a Marxist reply to that could be that the idea of nation is connected to the idea of capitalism, that nationhood was, let's say, the political expression of capitalism in its formative period. So that a socialist critique has always to be internationalist rather than nationalist. So the idea of asking socialists to construct a national ethic is somehow contradictory.

Grass: No, you see, the socialists, they make perhaps on Sunday a speech on internationalism, but all the week they are Polish or they are Russians. I don't believe in this. This is one of those theories of the 19th century that doesn't work any more.

Rushdie: Don't you think it's a curious paradox that in a way what happened is that capitalism became internationalist, you know, in the form of multinational companies or whatever it may be, that capitalism very skilfully developed techniques of internationalism, where socialism, in the form of trade union movements and so forth remained very parochial, very nationalistic, very confined inside the frontiers and so in a way what happened was the reverse of what was supposed to happen?

Grass: Yes, but I think that both ideologies, this kind of state capitalism called socialism in the East and our Western capitalism, they are run out, there is no more in it. And both ideas — capitalism came from the European Enlightenment, it was an answer to the medieval economic system, a hope for people, like socialism — belong together, but there are no more ideas coming from them and they are not able to give answers to these new kinds of questions.

Rushdie: So you would say that in a way there's a need for a kind of new Enlightenment or something of this sort?

Grass: Yes, if you look back to the beginning of the Enlightenment where reason was open enough to protect fantasy, to keep it inside, our understanding of reason did change after then, it became more and more short-minded. In the end we only have a technical understanding of reason, a very cold light is coming from this Enlightenment. And I think what what we need is a revision of our tradition of Enlightenment and to go back and make it richer again. I think it was a terrible mistake to blame human feelings and dreams as irrationalism. If you say this is not belonging to our modern understanding of Enlightenment, it will be very easy for the reaction, political reaction, to occupy these parts of our existence. And I think that literature can give an answer because the writer knows very well that reason is a small part of our existence from his knowledge, from his tradition, from his work, he knows very well how mixed up people are.

Rushdie: And you can make that mixing in the novel, in the text in the books, yes. I was very struck by a curious fact which I discovered which, in a way, showed me something about the reason why my writing had fallen towards this metaphorical, imaginative kind of writing, which is that I discovered that if you look etymologically at the meaning of the word metaphor and the word translation for example, it turned out they meant the same thing. See, translation from the Latin means to carry across. Metaphor from the Greek means to carry across. So again this comes back to my preoccupation with the idea of migration. People are also carried across, you see, so they're carried physically from one place to another. And I formed the idea that the act of migration was to turn people somehow into things, into people who had been translated, who had so to speak entered the condition of metaphor and that their instinctive way of looking at the world was in that more metaphorical, imagistic manner. Because then I was thinking that if you consider where the sense of ourself has always been located, the kind of places that it's been located are in the idea of roots, the idea of coming from a place, the idea of inhabiting a kind of language which you have in common, and the kind of social convention within which you live. And then what happens to the migrant is that they lose all three. They lose the place, they lose the language and they lose the social conventions and they find themselves in a new place, a new language. And so they have to reinvent the sense of the self, you know, and make it. So perhaps, because this is after all the century of the migrant as well as the century of the bomb, perhaps there have never been so many people who end up elsewhere than they began, whether by choice or by necessity, and so perhaps that's the source from which this kind of reconstruction can begin. People who are no longer caught in the old definition of the self, but capable of making new ones.

Grass: Yes, they learn it very early. But if you look around there are also people like a colleague of ours, Heinrich Böll, he was born in Cologne, he still lives there. Speaking with him he will tell you

that its not Cologne. It has changed so much he lost it years ago and
now there's another city. And we are really everywhere in the world
on a good way to destroy. To destroy in Germany, perhaps, a very
important part of our culture, the forests. You can't speak about
parts of German culture, like the romantics, without the forest
background of the fairy tales. They will soon be without any
background, then they are homeless. German fairy tales without
the forest can't exist. And you will find this mentality, this loss of
place all over the world.

CHAPTER 5

The New Cold War

Noam Chomsky and Fred Halliday

Noam Chomsky is one of America's most formidable intellectuals. In the mid-sixties, he revolutionised the study of Linguistics and at the same time emerged as one of the leading opponents of the Vietnam War and more generally of the exercise of American Global Power abroad. Since then, he has widely attacked the economic and military goals of U.S. foreign policy, reserving some of his fiercest criticisms for the subservience of intellectuals to the interests of the State. Most recently, Chomsky has written on the New Cold War, which he sees as one more chapter in America's attempt to control the Third World under the pretext of defending the West from Communism.

Fred Halliday is a leading writer on international affairs, one of the young British intellectuals who emerged with the new left in the sixties. Specialising in the Middle East, he has written mostly on the revolutionary changes that shook the region in the 1970s. Most recently, he's also one of the writers who have developed the idea of a New Cold War. But while emphasising the rivalry between the American and Soviet systems, Halliday presents a more global picture. In particular, he sees a clear relationship between superpower rivalry and conflicts in the third world, especially the wave of revolutions since 1974.

The New Cold War

Halliday: Noam, both you and I have written books on what we call the 'New Cold War' and we seem to agree on the fact that there is a new Cold War, a worsening of East-West relations and particularly, US-Soviet relations since the late Seventies. This is characterised by an increased arms race, by breakdown in substantial negotiations between East and West, but also by a change in climate within the two camps by an emphasis on ideological purity, whether it's on orthodox Marxism-Leninism in the Soviet Union or on conservative values in Britain and the United States, and by greater concern to martial control in the Third World, to control the allies — be it in Afghanistan on the one hand, or in the case of the United States, in Central America.

So we agree that just as there was a Cold War in the late forties and early fifties, so there seems to be a new Cold War now. But I also get the sense of some disagreement between us, that you lay much greater stress on control within the domains of each power. You say the United States and the Soviet Union are losing influence, have been losing influence over their respective allies since the sixties, or since the great days of the fifties for both of them, and that, in a way, they're using the Cold War rhetoric, they're using the idea of conflict between them, not to prosecute a conflict against each other, which I think in your view is largely mythical, or not so substantial, but to control the people who are subordinate to them. You've even said that the real enemy of the United States is not the Soviet Union so much as Japan, Western Europe, that they are seeking to control things.

In my view there is, of course, this element of controlling the situation at home, of Britain controlling its own population, the United States controlling its population, controlling the weaker allies in the Third World. But I give, I think, much more weight to the reality of the East-West conflict. I do think the United States and the Soviet Union have a lot to conflict about and that you can't understand this new Cold War if you don't see that the conflict has in fact got a lot of substance to it.

Chomsky: I think what the Soviet Union has wanted is essentially to be able to run their own dungeon without internal interference and to compete for influence in the Third World at targets of opportunity. The American version for world order has been much more expansive. And I think that essentially reflects the relative power of the two states, in particular immediately after the Second World War. The United States was in a position of global dominance which probably has no historical parallel and they were literally producing 50 per cent of world output and using roughly 50 per cent of world resources, and they knew it. They were conscious of it.

The United States has an extremely open society, nothing like it in the world. We have tons and tons of documentary evidence and it's very, very explicit. There was a very careful and explicit planning for the postwar world, and it was supposed to be a world which was going to be open to penetration and exploitation, by American-based, ultimately international corporations. Now the Soviet Union was plainly an impediment to that. First, by its existence. That is, it was simply not incorporated into what American planners called 'the grand area', the area subordinated to American influence. And secondarily, because it did support, to some extent at least, never to the extent claimed, but to some extent it provided some protection for movements towards independence elsewhere in the Third World, and that's an impediment. And in fact in the late forties and the early fifties, the United States was pursuing a rollback strategy. It was still hoping to break up the Soviet Union and incorporate it into the system.

But what I think has happened over the years is that the Cold War has increasingly come to have a certain functional utility for the superpowers. They can use it, it's useful for them, and I think that's a major reason for its persistence. It's not a zero sum game. It's not a competition in which one gains where the other loses. And I think you can see that by looking at the incidents of the Cold War. So, for example, if you take the Soviet Union, which has to mobilise its own population, as even a totalitarian state must do when it carries out aggressive or brutal actions, from the beginning, in fact from the intervention in East Berlin to the invasion of Afghanistan, it has always appealed to the threat of the foreign enemy. You know, the Americans standing there waving their missiles and carrying out savage acts, therefore we have to defend ourselves. And the United States has been doing the same thing from the beginning. I mean Acheson actually takes pride in his memoirs for his success in convincing Congress by a series of sheer deceptions that they had to move in on Greece and Turkey to defend themselves against the Russians. And that goes on up to the invasion of Grenada. You know, we invade Grenada — 'well, we have to defend ourselves from Russian attack.' Now that's been a very successful device for mobilising the American population for what are in fact acts of aggression and intervention.

There's a second factor too, which has to be emphasised, and that is that in the United States — maybe in the Soviet Union, but certainly in the United States — the military system has become essentially the technique of industrial policy management. If, when the Government has to intervene to subsidise high technology industry, as it repeatedly does, it does it through the military system. And in order to do that, you need a foreign enemy that you're defending yourselves against. Hence, you continually see in recent American history the conjunction of major military expenses, extended intervention overseas, and confrontationist tactics and appeal to the Russian threat. Now that's become an extremely useful system and we're locked into it, and I think it's a major reason for the persistence of the Cold War.

Halliday: I follow some of what you say, but I still don't agree. What you understate is two things: first of all, you understate the degree to which they still do dispute. In other words, this is not a stable competition, it is not — I think you once used the phrase 'a dance of death' in which each knows its place, its role and how far it can go. They do know how far they can go in terms of nuclear weapons and there haven't been many incidents, recently, or since the Cuban missile crisis, when the rules of the 'dance of death' have been unknown. But when it comes to the Third World, there really are not any rules and there's not any agreement on where they should stamp or not stamp.

I see the onset of the second Cold War from the late seventies onwards as a response by the United States, not just to disorder within their own realm, not just to lengthening queues of unemployed in Cleveland, Ohio, or to rebelling peasants in Nicaragua, but to the intersecting of revolt in the Third World, on the one hand, with Soviet power on the other. And that seems to me to be the history of the postwar world. Towards the end of the Vietnam war, from 1974 until the end of the seventies, there was a wave of Third World revolutions, by my count 14 countries, which went through Third World revolutions. There was Vietnam, there was Ethiopia, there was Iran — with very spectactular consequences — there was Central America and there were others. Now, these revolutions in themselves would support your view, they were revolts within the US domain, but at the same time they intersected with the conflict between East and West. Who was giving the Vietnamese the weapons to fight and kill Americans? Who was it who assisted the guerrillas in Africa, to weaken the Portuguese? Who was it who was encouraging Nicaragua, if not Cuba, and in some way the Soviet Union too?

Chomsky: In case after case, it has not been a major concern to American policy if a newly-independent area becomes allied to the Soviet Union. In fact, we drive them to do that, and in fact the United States even wants them to do that. You can see why. I mean, if we can drive Nicaragua into becoming a Cuban or Soviet client, that will give a justification for the further attacks that we intend to carry out to prevent them from extricating themselves from the world system that the United States controls. And you see — it's very striking — this is totally systematic, it happens in every case. In every case, if we cannot crush and destroy one of these revolutionary movements, we will act in such a way as to drive them into the hands of the Russians.

Halliday: If it happens in every single case, then surely it must be more than just the result of some bureaucratic conflict between hawks or doves, or Prussians and traders, to use Clare's expression. In other words, what you're suggesting is that in the case of each of these revolutions, China in the late forties, Cuba in 1959, Nicaragua in 1979, the planners in Washington really had an option: to live with them, to win them over, say 'we accept your revolution, we may not like it all, but we'll fund you,' and so forth, or to oppose them.

Chomsky: So these are major issues and they can go either way, but the policy, the choice has generally been the Prussian choice, to try to isolate and undermine the revolutionary government and to drive them into the hands of the Soviet Union as a justification for further attacks. That's been the general pattern. Grenada's a case, Guatemala was a case, and so on. Why? What is the threat posed by these countries? Well, it's not the threat that they're Russian outposts, it can't be that, because in fact we typically act in such a way as to make them Russian outposts. And in fact the United States is almost desperately trying now to turn Nicaragua into a Russian outpost.

So what is the real threat then, since that's not the threat? Why were they concerned about communist revolution? Well, the answer to that is also given. For example, it's given during an open document by a quite important study of the Woodrow Wilson Foundation in 1955, which is one of the major geopolitical analyses of the period. They say, perceptively, that the threat of communism is the inability or unwillingness of the communist powers to complement the industrial societies of the West. That is, the concern of communism is that it's autarchic, it uses resources for internal needs. So that's why we're always opposed to communism. What we care about is their subordination and integration into the grand area. So therefore, we'll be opposed to democracy in Guatemala, we'll be opposed to democracy in Chile, we'll be opposed to fascist regimes occasionally — if they're national fascists. The United States was opposed to national capitalism in Europe after the Second World War, opposed to mild socialism, and it'll be opposed to what's called communism crucially because communism was essentially correctly defined in that Woodrow Wilson study that I mentioned.

Any communist regime — I hate to use the term because I know it's nothing to do with anything that should intelligibly be called communist — what we call communist governments are, in fact, typified by their inability and unwillingness to become complementary to western industrial societies. Notice, incidentally, if they're willing to integrate themselves into the West, then we're sometimes willing to accept them, like contemporary China. But this is the thread that runs through everything. If we opened up trade with Nicaragua we would reduce the Russian penetration.

Halliday: But this is where I think you understate the reasons why in most cases the Prussians win. Or as we put it, in most cases, the militarists win and the hawks win, which is that Nicaragua, Algeria, many of these other cases, represent not just national control of the economy, not just independence, as you construe, but something more than that. They represent an alternative model of organising society, an alternative politics. And therefore the resistance, while it can be overcome in a few cases, goes to the heart of the American system. The American system of how a domestic polity should be run, the American view of how the world strategic and political structure of relations between states should be run, requires it to oppose, to crush, to try and roll back revolutions. If one looks at the conflicts between major world powers in the 19th century, between Britain and France, Britain and Russia, one can say that these were societies and polities which were organised in roughly similar ways but which were competing for territory, economic influence, strategic weight, and so forth.

Now, all of these elements are present in the rivalry between the United States and the Soviet Union, but there's something further, which is that these are societies and political systems which are organised in very different ways and which do present a threat to each other. Even though they exaggerate the degree of the threat, there is a real threat and both of them would like to gain ground at the expense of each other and, ultimately, eliminate the other from the face of the earth. The Russians would like to see a world organised in the way they're organised and the Americans would like to see American-style capitalism, their view of the free world prevail everywhere.

Now, of course, they live together because neither is powerful enough to overthrow the other and there is the small matter of nuclear weapons, which threatens the destruction of everything. So there are controls on this rivalry. But nevertheless, the rivalry has a deep reality to it. Their values are very different. People often say there is no cold war because nobody believes in communism and nobody believes in capitalism. Mrs Thatcher believes in capitalism, Ronald Reagan believes in capitalism, and I would have thought that Konstantin Chernenko believes in his view of communism as well. And they certainly believe in nationalism and in their nationalism being reflected in different social systems as well. So there is a conflict of values.

Secondly, I think that there is no doubt the societies are organised in a profoundly different way. As people in Russia often say 'if you think this is capitalism, you should come and look at it, it isn't capitalism.' There is no MacDonalds, there is no Bank of America, there is no Coca Cola advertisement on Kutuzovsky Prospect or Red Square in Moscow. And in the United States people are not given the kind of housing, social services, securities that people in the East have, and so forth. Power, wealth are organised and distributed in quite different ways in these countries and both of these systems have a hegemonic intent, hegemonic element. Thirdly, in the disputed area which is the Third World at the moment, but in the past was Europe and could become Europe again — in the Spanish Civil War and after the Second World War it was Europe — there is a competition for influence.

Now, we agree that the revolutionary upheavals in the Third World are not created by the Soviet Union, they're not dredged out of the blue by communist subversion or communist proxies or whatever the Cold War language might be, but that this rivalry between the two major powers and the two systems intersects with these insurrections in the Third World in a way that has a reality beyond the myths of rightwing propaganda. It may well be true that in 1954 Guatemala was not about to go into the Soviet camp, but the overall pattern of upheaval in the Third World since 1945 has been that many of these revolutions have turned to the Soviet Union, driven to them in some ways, but turned out of affinity in others — and affinity was very important in the Vietnamese case — and therefore the American refusal to accept these revolutions is not merely a policy mistake in the White House, it's not merely a refusal to accept independence or autarchy in general, it reflects, ultimately, the refusal to accept this alternative social system which is based on different values and a different system of organisation. And that's what lies at the core of the cold war.

Chomsky: Well, you see, I think part of what you say is true, but part of it in my view is simply mystical. The talk about alternative social systems and values, and so on, I think is a mysticism really.

Halliday: You say it's mystical to say the Soviet Union and the United States are different?

Chomsky: They're different, but that's not the problem. You get to the point when you say that there are no MacDonalds and there's no Pepsi Cola and so on and so forth. The existence of the Soviet Union is incompatible with the American view of world order because it is not freely open to penetration by American capital, its resources are not freely available.

Halliday: But Japan is not freely open to American capital.

Chomsky: Japan is very open, highly open, and where it is not open there is continual conflict. During and after the Second World War the United States planned a structure of world order, what the planners called 'the grand area' and that was to be, in their terms, the area stragically necessary for world control, the area that would be centrally subordinated to the needs of the American economy. But the point was that there had to be free possibility for export capital, for exploitation of resources, for investment overseas and so on. This region had to be open to American penetration and economic control, that's the crucial part. Now, the United States is not omnipotent but it has acted in such a way as to maximise these objectives.

If we look through the incidents of the Cold War, whether it's the rebuilding of European capitalism in terms which would be

integrated with, and in large part subordinated to the United States.
If we look at Middle East policy, if we look at Asia policy, if we look
at Central America Policy, we discover this unifying thread: always
the attempt to ensure that some region will not develop in such
a way that it will refuse to complement the industrial societies of
the West, primarily the United States. The United States has acted,
and will continue to act, to try to create a system in which what
they used to call in the 19th century 'free trade imperialism', will
work.

Vietnam: A Case in Point

Halliday: Much of what you've said so far suggests that the analysis
of the Vietnam war, both how it developed and also what it's
outcome was, is perhaps a central focus of the different ways in
which we look at postwar history. I mean, in my view, first of all the
whole development of the Vietnam war from the fifties, but
particularly since the serious American involvement from the late
fifties onwards, demonstrated that the view of the world of these
strategic planners was erroneous. That whatever they thought they
were doing about controlling the grand area, they did not
understand the forces involved. And that there was, in their
perception of Vietnam and in its strategic importance, a very clear
awareness that there was a conflict between the capitalist American
way of running the world and the Soviet communist way of running
the world, with the Chinese addition as well. That the war was not
just any old war in the Third World, it was a war between armies
representing very different social systems and indeed armies
organised in very different ways. And that the outcome of the war
was a very signal defeat for the United States. Not simply the only
major defeat the United States has ever suffered in a war, it greatly
weakened the United States economy internally and vis-a-vis its
competitors. And it sent a signal around the world to other
revolutionary movements that the United States could be defeated
by, as the Vietnamese would say, a combination of military,
political and diplomatic activity. It greatly encouraged the defeat of
the Portuguese colonies in Africa, it made possible the Cuban
intervention in Angola, it encouraged the revolutions in Central
America and so forth, and so it was a loss of American prestige as
well as of American life and of American treasure.

Of course the Vietnamese paid a terrible price, over 2 million
dead. Of course their society, their ecology have been terribly
damaged for decades, maybe hundreds of years. But nevertheless, a
country of 60 million people did defeat the United States. That
regime has consolidated itself, they've now of course, extended

their influence through the war with Cambodia to Cambodia itself, and in overall terms it was a major defeat for the United States. And nothing could illustrate this more clearly than the fact that even ten or more years after the last American troops left Vietnam there is still an enormous and healthy reluctance in the United States to send any troops abroad. For all that Reagan said in his first term about intervening in the Third World and overcoming the Vietnamese syndrome, all they could drum up was his pathetic *promenade militaire* in Grenada, which was of no military significance. The reason they had to pull their troops out of Lebanon was American public opinion wouldn't wash it. One of the major problems they have in sending troops to Central America is American public opinion, however bellicose it is, it won't buy it. So the Vietnamese not only defeated the United States inside Vietnam but they defeated the United States globally. And the impact of it is still with us. And I would see that as a very major development and a very major defeat for the United States.

Chomsky: Oh, I agree with everything you've said, and I think it's exactly half the story. Now, let's turn to the other half. Here we have to ask what the American goals were. And those we know very well from the documentary record I mentioned before. Let me repeat, the American policy with regard to Indo-China was set pretty well in the late 1940s and early fifties, within the general framework of grand area planning. An international order which will be open to the penetration of American-based enterprise and the exploitation of its resources and so on. That's the grand area, that's what we try to reconstruct. Why was Vietnam important? Vietnam was important, not for itself, there were virtually no American interests in Indo-China, despite some talk by Eisenhower about tin and tungsten, and so on, that was very minor. It was important within the framework of the domino theory. Now, I mean the rational domino theory. The theory was that an independent South Vietnam under so-called 'communist control' would carry out mass mobilisation and some degree of modernisation and industrialisation, leading to a social form which would be meaningful in terms of the Asian poor and could have a demonstration effect elsewhere — in Thailand, in Malaya, in Indonesia — ultimately leading to a system in which South-East Asia and South Asia would be extricated from the grand area under communist control. It could be a communism opposed to the Russians, or opposed to the Chinese, that didn't matter. It would be out of American control, not free, not open to, not part of the international capital system of exploitation and investment, and so on.

Then the next step, and it's the crucial step, would be the 'super domino' would fall, namely Japan. And Japan, which they always recognised would be the industrial centre of Asia, had its natural markets and sources of resources in this region, and would be forced to accommodate to it. And in effect, what we would have is a system like the one that Japan was attempting to construct in the 1930s, a new order, a system in large parts of Asia with an industrial Japan at its heartland, from which the United States would be excluded. And the United States was not prepared in the late 1940s to lose the Second World War. That was the picture that they had in mind.

Well, now let's look at the outcome. We talked about the negative effects for American policy, but there's another side. Vietnam is not going to have a demonstration effect which will lead to development of independent and successful peasant-based movements in Thailand, Malaysia and Indonesia. In Vietnam itself they didn't achieve their ends. Vietnam is not part of the American system, clearly, but in the region they achieved their ends. And the concern over Vietnam was a regional concern, it was not a Vietnamese concern. So therefore I think the conventional view, namely that the United States had suffered a defeat is partially true, but crucially only partially true, there was a regional victory.

The Arms Race

Halliday: Looking at the issue of intervention and what lies behind it, the new build-up of American power in the second Cold War, a question arises, which is this: is the build-up in American power, is the increase in military rhetoric, is the increased emphasis on strength and on American power, is the vastly increased military expenditure of the United States and its allies, can this be primarily explained by the Third World or not? Can it primarily be explained by the need to intervene in the Third World to discipline the grand area, which I would take to be your argument? Or has it not got a lot to do with the Soviet Union? Now my own view is this, that clearly the arms race serves multiple functions. It serves a domestic function, as we said earlier, the function of military Keynesianism, of boosting domestic expenditure. I still think it's different from military Keynesianism in the forties and fifties in that the effects are much more contradictory. It can have inflationary effects, it can draw people away from scarce employment and so forth. But nevertheless there is a military Keynesian effect for some sectors of the American economy and that's what the arms lobbies are all about in Washington. So there is a military-industrial complex which simply derives a domestic benefit. Fine. There is an ideological benefit. If you get people to believe in the army, if you raise the status of the army, if somebody walking down the street in a uniform is saluted and all the schoolchildren run after him, after her, as is currently the case in the United States, clearly that serves to strenghten conservative values. When it comes to foreign issues and to foreign purposes, and I would stress that in my view I think these are still the most important ones, I think we can't get away from the fact that the arms race, particularly the arms race as pursued by the United States, has, as common sense suggests it has, a primary target, which is the Soviet Union. In other words, it can't just be explained, the expenditure, the values, the propaganda about the arms race and the Soviet threat are not just about the Third World, and I would argue are not even primarily about the Third World, they point to the reality, the enduring reality of this East-West conflict.

Chomsky: Well, you see, I think each of the factors you've mentioned is real, but I think that you have failed to see the connection between them. I suspect that's where we primarily differ. I mean, I think you very much underestimate the military Keynesian effect. It's not a matter of the arms lobby.

Halliday: What, with the United States with the largest deficit in its history?

Chomsky: Yes, because this is a very costly means of industrial policy management. But nevertheless, for quite good reasons it's the only one we have. I'll come back to the reasons, but that's a fact, and it goes way beyond the arms lobby. So, let's take for example the development of computers. That's not the arms lobby. Now, in the 1950s the government was virtually the sole purchaser of computers. In the 1960s it was still purchasing, if I recall, up to about 50 per cent, and paying for the development. There's now a race for developing what they call 'fifth generation' computers. You know, super computers. Mainly with Japan, Europe is sort of out of it. Now, in Japan that's organised by their industrial management system.

Halliday: Nothing to do with the military.

Chomsky: It has nothing to do with the military. But how does it work in the United States? Well, the funding for super computer development is coming from the Pentagon, Research Project Agency of the Pentagon, from the Department of Energy, which is primarily a military department producing nuclear weapons, and from NASA, which is again largely a military organisation. The way in which the United States, for good historical reasons that we could go into, the fact is the way it organised industrial production, the way it develops high technology, that's the cutting edge of the economy, the way it encourages sunrise industry, is by creating a government-guaranteed market for high technology production and paying the research and development costs for it. Now, let's

turn to the second two factors, the Third World and the conflict with
the Soviet Union. They both exist, but I think you're wrong to
dissociate them. They're very closely related. And in fact again,
since the United States is an open society we can turn to the
documentary sources which explain the relationship. So, for
example, let's not talk about Reagan, as both you and I have
pointed out it was in the late Carter administration that a new phase
of the arms race developed, prior to the Iran hostages and prior to
Afghanistan. It was in '78 in fact that Carter offered his proposal for
the major increase in the military budget. In the last statement to
Congress of the Pentagon in the Carter administration, Harold
Brown, who was then Secretary of Defence, gave an explanation as
to why we have to have a big strategic weapons build-up. And the
way he put it, which is essentially correct, I think, is this: he said our
strategic weapons system is the foundation of our security, as he put
it, and he said within the framework of the strategic weapons system
our conventional forces become meaningful instruments of political
and military control. Now, that's correct.

Halliday: Why is Reagan launching this arms race?

Chomsky: Carter.

Halliday: And Carter. Why did Carter? And why did the
majority of the American people support it? Well, one reason is a
lot of nonsense about the Russians having military superiority,
which on any possible criterion except conventional forces in
Europe cannot be justified. One is that the Russians are more
powerful in the Third World, which is nonsense too. But
nevertheless, the arms race has this symbolic importance as being
the central symbol — nuclear weapons are the central symbol of
power, they are the potency symbol of international power for the
United States, and unfortunately for much of the US population as
well. Not unrelated to the fact that the United States has never had
any real experience of war. So there is this militaristic culture and
this militaristic association of power in which nuclear weapons are
very important. But there is also this control of the Third World, on
which we agree, and what percentage of the US budget goes for
intervention or how many of the arms, we can debate but that is
important. It's a central factor. And there is this third and
irreducible element of direct rivalry with the Soviet Union.

Chomsky: And what is the rivalry over?

Halliday: The rivalry is over Soviet power and the increase of
Soviet power. Both in terms of its geographical extent in the Third
World and also in terms of this symbolic element of how strong is
the Soviet Union?

Chomsky: But notice what we're agreeing on.

Halliday: Can I go on to say what we do agree on? And this is where you and I would disagree with many of those in the peace movement, is that the arms race, while it does have an irrational element, and while it is extremely dangerous is also in part motivated by rational political concerns. It is not out of control. It is not a Behemoth or a monster which is simply spreading and which human beings cannot control. It is not merely the product of a group of conspiratorial scientists or of secretive people in bunkers here, there and everywhere. It is a product of government decisions, of political decisions taken and repeated. And, at least in my view, and in your view, I think, in a different way, it is a product of a political and social conflict. And this cannot explain it completely, it cannot comprehend the moral horrors involved in this arms race, but we would put ourselves into a small minority of people who think that the arms race is controllable, is rationally explicable, and therefore can be rationally and politically controlled.

Truth and Power

Halliday: You've written a lot about the role of the intellectuals in society in general, but also in relationship to the foreign policy issues. You've been extremely critical of the way that mainstream intellectuals relate to foreign policy and the values of national power, while you yourself have sought to play a very different role as a critical intellectual, active in the peace movement, the anti-war movement and so forth, and in pioneering a different approach to foreign policy within the constraints that operate on you.

Chomsky: Well, my feeling is that to a very substantial extent the intellectual vocation has not been one guided by truth and honesty, but rather guided by service to external power. Now, this is not because there are bad people, there are very good institutional reasons for this. There are real rewards in any society, but in particular in rich Western societies, for accommodation to external power. And there are in fact rather harsh penalties for honesty and integrity, which lead to adopting positions which often conflict with those who really have economic and political and sometimes even physical power in the societies in question. So what you tend to find, and I think this is a very general phenomenon, but in our society it works too, what you tend to find is a continual subordination to the demands of external power. And it shows up in all sorts of ways. So, for example, in the American foreign policy literature the framework is one of containment. You know, response. The United States is not inactive, it responds to the evil deeds of others, sometimes unwisely. The problems are held to appear in Vietnam or the Middle East or Central America, our violent neighbours. What is missing almost entirely is a recognition of the fact that the problems of those regions are to a very substantial extent problems rooted in American institutions and their systematic behaviour and functioning over the years. The role that they end up playing, the ones who achieve a degree of success, is to provide an ideological framework, which makes at least them and tries to make the general population support this.

There's nothing very sophisticated about it. It's very simple and concrete. Take, say, the Vietnam war again. Now, this is a very dramatic example, I think. Let me compare the Vietnam war with the Russian invasion of Afghanistan. There are plenty of differences but there are some similarities. One similarity is that the Russians invaded Afghanistan and the Americans invaded South Vietnam. Now, in the Western system, including the United States, everyone recognises that the Russians invaded Afghanistan, nobody doubts that. But there is virtually no recognition of the fact that the United States invaded South Vietnam. In fact, in 1962, that's now 23 years ago, Kennedy began bombing South Vietnam. American troops began bombing South Vietnam in 1962. They began massive defoliation. That was part of a campaign to drive several million people into concentration camps, where we would separate them from the guerrillas who we admitted they were willingly supporting. Now, that's an invasion, that's an attack. It was stepped up to a bigger invasion years later. Let's imagine, let's say 25 years from now or 20 years from now, no one in the Soviet Union has ever referred to a Russian invasion of Afghanistan, suppose they've only referred to a Russian defence of Afghanistan which some people —

Halliday: A limited contingent, is the official phrase.

Chomsky: Whatever. But a defence which was maybe unwise or too bloody or something like that. Well, you know we would regard that as a miracle of totalitarian thought control. But we're living in the midst of that miracle and we don't see it. You know, here we're living in the middle of a victory of something like totalitarian thought control that very dictators could boast of. Now that's not an unusual example. There are many such cases. I've in fact written probably by now thousands of pages of documentation on cases exactly like that. The net effect of course is zero. Because there are good functional reasons why this happens. You cannot function as a successful Western intellectual, with statistical error apart, I mean a few people can, but basically you can't function unless you accept the doctrinal system which says the United States and the West in general are basically benevolent in intent, defensive in purpose, responsive to the acts others. You know, noble aims. occasionally making mistakes and so on and so forth. That's the framework of thinking you must adopt.

Halliday: Yes.

Chomsky: Now, one thing that you said before which I thought was crucially important is that while this system was very effective in disciplining the population up till the middle 1960s, it began to break down in the late 1960s. I mean, the reality of Vietnam was so obvious that you just couldn't maintain this system for a large part of the population. And incidentally, the opinion polls are rather striking on this in what they reveal. For example, as recently as 1982, up till the present almost — there's a Gallup Poll does a sample of opinions on all sorts of topics every year — and in 1982, the most recent on I've seen, they asked the question, as they always do, about attitudes towards the Vietnam war and the answers are kind of revealing. People were asked was the Vietnam war a mistake or was it fundamentally wrong and immoral? Well, in the population as a whole 72 per cent said fundamentally wrong and immoral, not a mistake. Among people they call 'opinion leaders' it was much lower. And among the articulate intelligensia it was virtually zero. Among the articulate intelligensia, at the peak of anti-war opposition, around 1970, there were maybe five per cent or so who were willing to say it's more than a mistake. Now that's a radical break between what we might call the Commissars and the people that they're supposed to discipline. And a major task for the intelligensia in the 1970s has been to try to overcome that.

Halliday: So you see the task of the American intelligensia as disciplining the population as a whole to accept the legitimacy of the Vietnam war and say that it was a mistake rather than being fundamentally wrong?

Chomsky: That's one. I mean, much more generally they want to discipline the population to accept a similar view with regard to the exercise of American power altogether.

Halliday: One thing though that strikes me as a problem is this: if we take as our starting point that we're living in developed capitalist countries, we're trying to criticise the foreign policies of our own governments while at the same time trying to encourage those who are wanting to be less dependent on the Soviet Union. We want, in other words, to create a space in between the blocs in which people can be more independent, more democratic and so forth. One faces a choice about how to focus one's limited time and efforts. Now, I think your work has tended to focus on the critique of American foreign policy and the critique of what intellectuals write and what the press and the media write. And you've done this very effectively. But there strike me as being two problems there. One is almost a theoretical point, which is this: how do you refute the arguments of the other side? Now, you've chosen, as I see it, to refute them by pointing up the inconsistencies, the misuse of evidence, the moral foreshortenings that go on. But I'm doubtful about whether one gets very far with doing this. My sense, and what I've tried to do in my own work, is not to spend an awful lot of time criticising what the press or the academics write about anything, but is to offer one's own alternative explanation of the Cold War, of Third World revolution, of the development of Iran, or whatever it might be. In other words, the best way to rival them is not by burrowing away trying to show how wrong they are but to provide an alternative explanation. Secondly, if you set yourself up as being frontally opposed to and criticising imperialist ideology or the dominant ideas as they relate to Third World conflicts you fall into the trap, or you may do, of underestimating those problems which are not the result of imperialism but may be due to the savagery of revolutionary groups, or may be due to the backwardness of the country or whatever. And we've seen enough revolutions in recent years where there've been a lot of problems, remotely a product of imperialist bombardment or the feudalism, whatever it might be, but not just to do with that, with the way in which revolutionaries actually handle their own population. And you've obviously been open to some criticism on this score, that by focusing uniquely on the lies, distortions, moral partialities of mainstream writing you've not given enough attention to what others have done in the Third World, which is nothing to do with imperialism.

Chomsky: Well, it may be that my choices are not the ones that should be taken. But let me explain what they come from. First of all, as to the second question, my own attitude towards — I've continually indicated here that I'm reluctant to use words like 'communism,' 'revolution' and so on and so forth. I'm not a great afficionado of revolutionary movements. In fact, I think they're mostly pretty brutal. I don't think they have anything to do with socialism, and this includes the Bolshevik revolution, which in my view is disastrous. I mean, my feeling is these movements should be allowed to take their own course. We neither have the authority nor the confidence to rule them. You know, nobody appointed us God. They're going to have to find their way to solve their own problems.

Halliday: No, but we can write about them and write about them in a critical way.

Chomsky: We can write about them, and I do write about them in fact, but I don't consider it my main task. I've explained what I think is the nature of these movements, going back to their origins in Leninism and in fact in Marxism, and I don't regard it as a main focus of my talk to point out how this is true here, here, here and the other place. Now, why don't I? Well, the reason is that I don't find it particularly useful to march in parades.

Halliday: But if you, as you put it, march in the parade, if you criticise people whom the *Wall Street Journal* or the *New York Times* also criticise, you do so in a very different way, with a different moral authority, and in fact you don't give to them the monopoly of criticising these events.

Chomsky: Well, no, that's not true. I do in fact repeatedly, in my own writing and elsewhere, discuss the nature of these revolutionary movements.

Halliday: All right, but I wanted to get at this phrase 'I don't march in parades,' because you might have ended up saying, you know, 'in 1937 everybody was denouncing the Moscow trials so I'm going to keep quiet about it.' Which I don't think is your position.

Chomsky: No, I mean, I would denounce the Moscow trials in 1937. In fact, in 1937 it was different, because then there was a substantial part of the intelligensia that wasn't denouncing the Moscow trials and in fact was defending them. We have to remember that, for example, George Orwell's *Homage to Catalonia* couldn't even be published in the United States in 1938. So that's different. Today, for example, I write critically of the Russian invasion of Afghanistan, but I'm not going to bother writing an article about it just repeating what's in the popular press. I've nothing to add about that. What I consider it to be useful to do is to provide information and analysis and, I hope, understanding that is different from what is readily available. What I want to do is identity problems that are first of all important and morally significant, that is there are human consequences to what we do or don't do about them, and that are badly misunderstood and misinterpreted. Those are the topics I want to consider.

Halliday: Looking back on it, do you think what you wrote about Cambodia, both before and after the Vietnamese invasion, was balanced? Do you feel happy with that, or are there some things you'd wish to change?

Chomsky: No, I wouldn't change anything. In fact, there's very little change because I wrote virtually nothing. It's kind of interesting that people think I've written about this topic when in fact I didn't. It's part of the reconstruction of ideology in the West, part of the attempt —

Halliday: Hang on, you did talk about Western hysteria over the killings.

Chomsky: All right, let's get the facts straight. I wrote one review, book review, period, during the period —

Halliday: No, you talked about hysteria after.

Chomsky: That's after. Okay?

Halliday: And you said one thing which I must say did strike me. I mean, let's face it, you never denied that massacres took place in Cambodia.

Chomsky: Not only did I not deny them, I stressed them.

Halliday: So I think that the bottom line is that a lot of what you're supposed to have said about Cambodia you never said. What you did say before and after, you stick by now.

Chomsky: Absolutely.

Halliday: Because it fits into this general picture of criticising.

Chomsky: Okay, so that's a very interesting case. What we said about the whole situation, Vietnam and Cambodia, and in a book that came out after the Pol Pot regime we documented this in tremendous detail. So people can look it up if they're interested in it. There's a couple of hundred pages of documentation about it and nobody's ever, to my knowledge, found anything wrong with it. What we showed is that the farther you got away from the source, the harsher the criticisms got.

Halliday: Yes.

Chomsky: Okay, so we said from the people who were directly observing as much as one can, from refugees, we are getting one sort of picture. The people who are commenting on them are giving a harsher picture. The people that are commenting on them are giving a still harsher picture. And in fact the farther you go away from the direct reports the more gruesome and awful it appears. We furthermore pointed out, and this is also correct, that there was quite a distribution of actual reports. So, for example, the *Far Eastern Economic Review* and American intelligence and so on were giving different reports than those that appeared from other people. And we thought those should be looked at. They were in fact saying that there were obviously major atrocities but they were not anything like the scale of what was being claimed. So, for example, State Department intelligence in 1977 held that there were tens or hundreds of thousands of people who had died from all causes, primarily from starvation and disease, for which incidentally the American war bears not a small responsibility I should say. And it was harsh and brutal and oppressive, they said, but not mass genocide. That was the picture of State Department intelligence in 1977.

I felt then and feel now that State Department intelligence is worth taking seriously. They're the people who knew most about the situation, and furthermore let me point out that in retrospect they turn out to be accurate. We now know a lot about that. We know a great deal about it. We probably know more about Cambodia from '75 to '79 than any other period in Cambodian history. And what is now known is that the State Department intelligence analysis was correct. The story about Pol Pot carrying out mass genocide at that time, 1977, was simply not correct.

Starting in about 1977 or '78 there was a major effort in the West to do two things. First of all, to show that what happened in Cambodia, the atrocities in Cambodia, were an indication that we must oppose every revolutionary movement everywhere. So, for example, Carter's Ambassador to El Salvador, and that's in a year in which the United States was backing and organising massacres which in fact bear comparison to the Pol Pot massacres, he accused the Left, the guerrillas, of being what he called a 'Pol Pot Left.' Now that's in reference to the groupings based ultimately on church-based organisations and unions and peasants and so on that the United States was interested in slaughtering.

Halliday: Well, the El Salvador guerrillas have eliminated quite a few of their own number as well. But not on the scale of Pol Pot.

Chomsky: They killed people, but to say that this grouping was the 'Pol Pot Left' was not only ludicrous but particularly vicious when in fact we were carrying out actions that maybe could be compared to Pol Pot.

Halliday: Okay, so you're talking about the function.

Chomsky: That was the function. All right, secondly, along with that came a pretence, which is kind of comical in fact, that there were people defending Pol Pot. You had to also undermine the peace movement. You have to undermine the critical movement. And the way of undermining it was to pretend that it was defending Pol Pot, it was defending these huge atrocities. Now, the fact of the matter is that there was nobody defending Pol Pot outside of some very marginal Maoist sects. There was literally nobody defending Pol Pot. You can't find anyone.

Halliday: In what did the Western hysteria over massacres in Cambodia consist? I mean, you used the word hysteria.

Chomsky: First of all there was huge publicity given to them. There was vast exaggeration of their scale on very flimsy evidence.

Halliday: It's a bit like saying people got hysterical about Hitler, he only killed 30 million, not 100 million. But there was a major problem there.

Chomsky: There's a value to truth. Truth has a value, I think. And I think facts matter. So in fact it matters whether there was a co-ordinated central campaign to massacre three million people or whether in fact a peasant revolution went wild and there were sectors in which massive killings took place and there were other sectors in which they didn't take place and it was complicated and so on and so forth. These facts matter. And it's worth telling the truth about them to the extent that one can.

Now, in the late seventies there wasn't very much you could say, because not too much was known. But what was said, what reached the public, whether it was in the *Reader's Digest* for the masses or in the *New York Review* for the elite, was that that there was a co-ordinated massacre carried out by Marxist-Leninists that was murdering two million or three million people and was the worst thing since Hitler and so on and so forth, and that any questioning of this was illegitimate. Now that's on a par with for example, it matters whether the United States carried out germ warfare in Korea in the early fifties. If somebody says 'well, I don't think the evidence is good enough,' that's not apologetics for the United States. You know, truth matters.

CHAPTER 6

What Became of the Boys?

Heinrich Böll and Kurt Vonnegut

Heinrich Böll is one of Germany's most distinguished writers. Brought up during the unrest of the twenties and thirties, his youth was dominated by nazism and the war. He served in the German army for six years and was captured by US forces in the Spring of 1945. The war was a decisive influence on his writing and his first stories and novels are significantly set in the years of retreat and defeat after 1943. In a clear, precise prose he described the absurdity of war and the need to face up to the ethical legacy of nazism. His later writing probes the conscience and values of postwar Germany, speaking out against complacency and materialism. Perhaps more than any other writer he has been the humane conscience of modern Germany and in 1972 he was awarded the Nobel Prize for literature.

Kurt Vonnegut is one of America's leading contemporary novelist. Like Böll, he belongs to that generation of writers who grew up in the Depression and fought as enlisted men during the Second World War. While Böll was in an American prisoner-of-war camp, Vonnegut was captured by the Germans and sent to Dresden, where he witnessed the fire bombing that completely destroyed the city. This tragedy later became the subject of his most famous novel, *Slaughterhouse Five*. His early work was mainly science fiction, but as he came to prominence in the sixties the war featured more profoundly in his writing. Since then he has mixed genres and subjects freely, always writing with humour and compassion, more concerned with humane values than social conventions.

Böll: My idea, Kurt, about comparing biographies, comes from the wish to understand people and I think to compare biographies of people of about the same age internationally would make it easier for us to understand their behaviour, political developments, their revolutions. Imagine you were born in Germany in 1922, what would become of you?

Vonnegut: Well, Günter Grass told me that everyone my age is dead. That there is no male for me to talk to in Germany who was born in 1922. But I have written that I, in fact, if I had grown up in Germany, at no point would I have become a dissident that I can see it, starting with the youth organisations, and only about half-way through the war would I have realised that I had been grossly swindled. But I've also said that I would have been dumb enough to go to the Vietnam war. Out of curiosity. Out of a feeling it's a citizen's duty, if his neighbours are going to war, I should go too. None of my children did. Because I had four healthy sons. But that was their business. I would have been dumb enough to go.

Böll: But in Germany you would have functioned?

Vonnegut: I think so.

Böll: Joined the army, fought the Russians?

Vonnegut: Yes, I would. I think I was —

Böll: I did. I did. I functioned too.

Vonnegut: I was very lucky to grow up in the United States rather than Germany. I might easily have grown up in Germany as I had a first cousin who did. And who was in the Wehrmacht. And when we met years ago I think I told you that he shot himself. He was on the Russian front, and by the time he got back to the hospital the wound couldn't be found. He was in no need of treatment. But he has a sense of being had, being swindled. But his mother did not. His mother just died in Indianapolis, where she grew up. She married a German when she was about 20 years old and lived in Hamburg. She still sees the Second World War as a great athletic event. Where the Germans, against enormous odds, fighting on many fronts all over the world, outnumbered on all of them, held them off for an amazing length of time.

Böll: Still does?

Vonnegut: Well, she's dead, but that's what she thought up to the moment she died. And I was never able to shake her.

Böll: In spite of the defeat and the total demoralisation of the German army? Because I functioned without conforming. Because there was no choice. You would go into a concentration camp or prison and could die very easily there. I was caught. So I joined the army, but I never was conformed with the regime. And I wonder what have would have become of me if I had been born in America in 1917. I probably would have joined the American army to fight the Germans.

Vonnegut: Well, more than that, you would have had no sense of being a German yourself. Because the German Americans gave up on being German Americans.

Böll: Germans easily do.

Vonnegut: And, well I can remember that my father was fluent in German as I am not, and he was the third generation to be born in the United States. But he gave up on speaking German around our house during the First World War. But he had no sense of being anything but an American. And we are the largest wave of migration to the United States after the Anglicans, the Germans. And then the next most numerous were the Irish and the next most numerous were the Italians. But one American in four has a German ancestor now.

Böll: And they function very well?

Vonnegut: They have no sense of being Germans. One thing that was very convenient in a way is that we had a word to substitute for German, which was nazi.

Böll: Nazi, yes.

Vonnegut: They were lucky that there was that name to attach to a fleeting nightmare.

Böll: For the whole German people, yes.

Vonnegut: So once it ceased to be a nazi government, I mean on May 8th, when the war ended, there was this sudden cleansing process. Suddenly they weren't nazis any more, they were Germans again. But in two world wars there are no spying scandals associated with German Americans.

Böll: But identification, nazi and German ended with the end of the war?

Vonnegut: Well you started looking for the real nazis. It seemed you could separate them out. You could arrest them.

Böll: But we were all nazis in a way.

Vonnegut: Well, yeah, but —

Böll: I was called a fucking German nazi too.

Vonnegut: For how long?

Böll: Oh, for half a year. And I understood it. I understood it. I understood the feeling of an American coming to fight in Germany.

Vonnegut: I was in the American army, you were in the German army, and certainly the posters on my barracks walls and the movies I saw gave every indication that you were really quite subhuman. And the whole nation believed this.

Böll: But the strange thing is that our propaganda, German, was only anti-Soviet.

Vonnegut: That I didn't know. I didn't know that.

Böll: Not much propaganda against British or American. There were jokes about Churchill drinking and so on, but the main propaganda — and that is the reason still for anti-Soviet feeling in Germany — was against Eastern European people: Polish people, Russian people, Jewish people within those countries. And I had the opportunity to read before I went to war. I read Russian literature so I wasn't infected very much by this propaganda. But I have the impression that most people are infected by this kind of propaganda.

Vonnegut: It is exciting. I have said that hatred is like vitamins. You do feel better. And there are people who go around in a considerable state of excitement, more alert than you and I are usually. They're really wide awake and there's a spring to their step and all that because they are really angry with somebody, or really frightened by someone.

Böll: Personally?

Vonnegut: Yes.

Böll: By propaganda?

Vonnegut: Yes, but businessmen will get very angry at their competitors. I worked for General Electric for a while, as did our President Ronald Reagan, and we were encouraged to hate Westinghouse, which was the second largest electrical manufacturer in the United States.

Böll: It was your enemy.

Vonnegut: Yes, and every morning when we came to work we were deeply offended by any favourable comment on Westinghouse in the newspaper.

Böll: Imagine President Reagan born in Moscow in 1910. What would become of him? What do you think?

Vonnegut: Well this is interesting to project. I don't know how much work there is for actors there. He would be a good boy in any society.

Böll: Most Russians are good boys in their society.

Vonnegut: And if he had been born in Germany, well, he's five years older than you, something like that. He's in fine condition. He would have been an officer in the SS or would have hoped to be, I think. To achieve a certain amount of rank and wear one of those —

Böll: I think he would become an actor in Moscow in 1930, when he was 20. And then, if he was a really good boy he would have joined the army, he would have fought the Germans and been proud of it. Is it too difficult for him to displace himself into Moscow, into Leningrad or any other Russian city? Well, to understand what's going on in this great continent east of us —

Vonnegut: We would have to..

Böll: That good boys are good boys everywhere, everywhere. Working and functioning what the governments want of them. Maybe he would become a colonel in the army. I don't know.

Vonnegut: Well, what we would have to do with Reagan, who is an actor, is we would have to write him a script, and then if we were to make a sympathetic movie about a first lieutenant in the Russian army in the Second World War, then he would understand. And he has never made such a movie, he has never had such a script. But, as I say, he and I worked for the General Electric Company at the same time, the same department, advertising and publicity. We never met. But he was hired to speak for General Electric. He wasn't getting movie parts then. So he's handed a new script on a subject he had probably never thought about before, the evils of public power generation, you know, as opposed to privately-owned power and light companies.

Böll: He would play his role.

Vonnegut: Of course.

Böll: And he would have played his role in the Soviet Union too.

Vonnegut: Yes.

Böll: Would he become a dissident?

Vonnegut: No, surely not.

Böll: I don't think so.

Vonnegut: Surely not.

Böll: That's very important to know. I don't understand this development between the United States and Soviet Union after the war. I think it started even before the war ended. This thing of feeling a new enemy after the nazis were dead and gone. And a lot of Germans were very cooperative with the Americans. The most cooperative people in Europe are the Germans for the United States. And most of them were nazis. That's very difficult to understand for me. That the old enemy — we are not a nazi country, we are the Federal Republic of Germany, a real democracy, all right — but this ability of cooperation one must feel dangerous too. I think they are too cooperative, the Germans. Now. As they were cooperative with the nazis too.

Vonnegut: And your books again and again and again deal with people leading their own lives, as following their own instincts regardless of the opinion of neighbours and all. And I have fantasised about if I had grown up in Germany, as to how I would have weathered this, as to how much of a life I could have salvaged out of these nightmare years. Which would have been a little love making, I suppose, and a little drinking and a cigarette now and then. These very primitive pleasures while I'm in the midst of a world gone mad.

Böll: That was my idea when I was a prisoner of war, became a prisoner of war, that there was not much chance of a life out of slavery. That was my fear and my expectation too. So I felt we in the Federal Republic of Germany, we came off too well after that war. You know what I mean? We did suffer with hunger like the whole of Europe did. And Holland and France and Britain and all. And it was a hard time up to 1949 or so. But looking back, seeing what damage the Second World War did, we came almost out as victors. That makes me feel in a strange position as a German, you know. I feel strange anyway in this world, and that's a metaphysical question, but this is a political and geographical question, and that's my suspicion, that we are spoiled for certain reasons. And I would like the reason.

Vonnegut: Well I know one reason is we wanted very much your infantry. I mean, I said to you recently that I thought that the

German army was without question the greatest army in history. It was the most efficient and the most wily.

Böll: I don't agree.

Vonnegut: You don't believe this. But Americans believe this. I mean, when I was in the American infantry I had a feeling I was fighting professionals really and we weren't really nearly as good at this game as the Germans were. And we really did want your infantry, what we could salvage out of it. And I think we have the dream right now that the Germans are so tough and know so much about fighting that they could slow the Russians down.

Böll: The Germans to the front. I think it's an error, I think it's an error but you can talk about it.

Vonnegut: But then you'll have the punishment you seek, you see. We intend to punish Germany in a very useful way in the front line. Well what else do we have to count on? If you're not going to stop the communist menace, who is?

Böll: I wouldn't trust the German army in that way.

Vonnegut: When I was a prisoner of war, and finally when it was evident the war was over and we could hear the Russian guns and it was time for our guards to simply disappear. The last thing they said to us is 'all right, now you're going to have to fight the Russians'.

Böll: Yes, there were some American officers going round German prisoner camps asking 'what would you do if we would fight the Russians now?' in May-April 1945, and the standard answer was 'I would go to church and pray for victory'. But nobody would say for whose victory. That was the standard answer of the German soldier in the prisoner camp. Nobody wanted to fight again. And it was a demoralised army.

Vonnegut: But at the same time we saw finally nazis who weren't shooting at us any more and they were just there in the open surrendering, not fighting any more and the submarines were surfacing and the crews giving up and all that and we finally got a good look at the enemy who'd been dug in so well. At the same time we discovered the death camps which was quite new and startling. We'd heard rumours of these things, but very little was said about them and I don't think we believed strongly that they did exist to the ordinary American citizen, but simultaneous with the German surrender were these camps and they were so horrifying that there was no possibility for simultaneous sympathy for the defeated army. If it hadn't been for those camps I think there would have been a great deal of sympathy of the sort my aunt would have liked, because you fellows really fought awfully well on a lot of fronts and were frequently outnumbered and all of that.

Böll: But it was one part of the liberation. And the Russians liberated a lot of camps too. It was my trauma for years — still now

— to go into shower baths and when I saw the first pictures of the great concentration camps, Auschwitz — shown by the American army — I was so frightened that I couldn't come out of the shower. I waited 20 years or more to go into a shower bath after the war. It's still difficult for me. I'm sure that British hotels or bathrooms spray gas on me. It's a trauma, this, and one experience I'll never forget. And there is a great discussion now in Germany, as you know probably, about how to feel about the end of the war and I made a report out of it, my feeling, and my feeling was that of liberation through the American army absolutely. The expectation of how they would go on with and deal with us was a different one. The first and main impression was liberation from the internal nazi terror in Germany which is not yet described. Himmler was the main person, Himmler, not Hitler, Hitler was far away talking nonsense like Goebbels, absolute executive power completely was in Himmler's hands, so it was internal terror within Germany.

Vonnegut: What were the dates? From when to when?

Boll: It was after the 20th July, after the *Attentant* of the officers. This development after July '44 up to the end of the war was growing internal terror. Everybody could denounce everybody and you wouldn't know who is a denouncer or who not. I was a deserter at the time. It was difficult days, a lot of deserters were hanged and shot and I went back to the army to save my life because it was the safest way, became a prisoner. Full of the propaganda of the Morgenthau plan, I didn't expect much for myself.

Vonnegut: This was to turn Germany into an agricultural nation right? To destroy all Germany industry.

Boll: Yes, it wouldn't have been the worst, but I expected slavery for at least 10 years in Soviet Union or France or Great Britain because by the German war whole of Europe was in destruction. All right, but then I was released very early from prisonership in October '45.

Vonnegut: You were an American prisoner of war?

Boll: Yes, in a big camp of 200,000. It was not nice but, all right, I didn't expect it to be nice. I came home. I was sick, weak for two years, not interested in politics because I thought they will deal with it anyway. But in '47-48 there started a new political life in Germany with different parties, different programmes, and I became interested in that and had the hope, and there was reason for that hope, that Germany would become a sort of Christian socialist country. So my expectation after I had forgotten Morgenthau and all that was that we would become a neutral unmilitary country within Europe. This hope held on up to the beginning of the fifties when the remilitarisation came. And the hope is diminishing, you know, from day to day with developments within Germany. And what was your expectation? You were younger, I was 32 when I became a new political consciousness, you were 23?

Vonnegut: Yes I was 23 when I got out of the army, 22 or 23, and in a way my postwar story is quite silly. Because I came from such a rich country which took such light casualties, in fact, as very few of us were killed, and also we weren't attacked at all except for Hawaii and so we came home with all the feelings that homecoming soldiers have. We had fought in a just war, perhaps the only one the United States ever engaged in, but we had every reason to have excised this political cancer which Germany had become. We bred as though we had had enormous casualties. We had this biological experience: as the boys are coming home we must replace the casualties by copulating and creating. Without having lost many people in the field, we still behaved as though we had and so we had the largest generation of children in the history of the country. It caused us to build many new schools and all that sort of thing because we all came home and had children instantly. But we were rich and my dream was largely materialistic, because after all I already belonged to a utopia of considerable age, as we had lived under the United States constitution which is the best thinking about human freedom distilled from thousands of years of literature and thinking about justice. So we already lived under a quite sane form of government, so we saw no reason to improve anything, except the economy, and when we came home there was work for everyone. My dream was materialistic, I'd come out of the depression, that was the great event in my life, not the war. All industry had stopped and my father had no work and we had no money and bill collectors and all that, and that was the large experience in my life, as, of course, it was in Germany too and in France and in the whole world. But my dream was materialistic, after the war is over I will get a house, I will get a car, I will have a couple of babies and we will take vacations, and that all came true.

Böll: We had no Germany. No possibility of materialistic dreams. We went back to Cologne absolutely destroyed, 30,000 inhabitants after 780,000 living in the middle of the ruins. Our children were born there. Our sorrow was very elementary: to get food, not to starve. Daily fighting for anything to eat and to have a flat, building a flat of your own. And my ambition was to write, even when I was 20, and I started writing in the middle of the ruins. My wife was a teacher, she earned money. Our only hope was really — it sounds very pathetic, full of pathos — a new Germany, you know, after the experience of the nazi time and after the defeat. And the feeling of being a German, you may imagine what it meant in 1945.

Vonnegut: When did things start getting better? When was there enough food? How soon after the war was there finally enough to eat and some place to live?

Böll: Oh it was about '50-51. It took five years. Our children didn't suffer, that was the main thing. We had friends and we helped each other. We went on the black market if we had some money and so we came along, we survived. Let's call it that, we survived, and it was the main thing.

Vonnegut: Would you trade cigarettes for food or food for cigarettes?

Böll: No, I traded food for cigarettes in the American prison camp. We didn't get cigarettes, they were not allowed, not one, and there was a black market within the camp and you had to give one day's ration which was quite a lot, not materially a lot, but for survival, for one cigarette. So we put three together, each gave a third of his ration and he got a third of a cigarette. We smoked it very intensely, it was like opium, because it's relative, most like having a very, very strong joint. To put a third of a cigarette on a needle to inhale it up to the very last you know.

Vonnegut: Yeah when I was a prisoner of war I traded my food ration for cigarettes and I was wondering — we're both notorious chain smokers still, against the best advice of medical science — and I'm amazed that I would trade a piece of bread, half a loaf of bread or whatever the ration was, for a damned cigarette. And it was clearly worth it, I never questioned the deal afterwards or felt what the hell did I think I was doing?

Böll: Cigarettes were the real money, all things were counted with cigarettes.

Vonnegut: You could borrow them too. You could borrow a cigarette today if you promised to give back two cigarettes tomorrow.

Böll: No you couldn't. For a heavy smoker, it was a bad time, very bad time, and that was not the real trouble. The real trouble was to be a German, waiting for a new Germany to be built by new political powers. And later I found out that the generation between 30 years old and 20 which would be normally building a new society was almost all dead, or sick or emigrated. You know a lot of Germany emigrated, and it was not the worst part of Germany. Sometimes when I meet friends, emigrees, old emigrees in New York or England or Israel — not only Jewish people — I have the feeling they are the real Germans. That's the Germans I lived with. We changed a lot, Germany changed so quickly, so rapidly and you couldn't imagine how many times better some people are off than they were before the war. If I go to villages I knew from my childhood walking or biking, wandering about, I can't believe it. The real German economic miracle takes place in the countryside because you see new quarters with big villas and cars, I don't know where they come from. Now, after the fifties, early fifties, it became clear that we would have an army again and they needed the old nazi generals. It was a real revitalisation of nazism. Not nazism in the form of ruling, but mentally. That was a very important time for the development of Germany, the early fifties. Our hope for a real Christian socialist Germany is gone forever.

Vonnegut: Well militarism is very exciting to the United States too. The great change that I saw when I was going to primary school and to high schools up until the time I was 18, America was a pacifistic nation and I was in a publicly-supported school system and we were told to be proud that we did not have a large standing army and Germany and the Soviet Union and France had these hundreds of thousands of people under arms and also military officers wearing their uniforms held cabinet positions. We had no such people and so the United States was militarised against its will, against what used to be its basic nature by Japan and Germany, by the threat to those two large markets of ours, finally, was that we had to get a big army too.

Böll: But coming back to our expectations, after the war certainly the Germans wanted food and drink and a flat and a bed to sleep in, materialistic things which is normal and elementary, but the deep trauma to us was two total inflations. You know what a total inflation is? That your money is nothing. And when I was a child my father went to his workshop in the morning by bike and he gave me a bill of a billion marks for a piece of sugar or bon bon — a billion.

Vonnegut: Who would give you a piece of sugar for that?

Böll: He worked for the small fortune, he had a hard life and it was nothing, after the First World War. And then we had a stable mark, a *Rentenmark*, *Reichsmark* — it became 24 years old, it died very young. Nothing again. For a hundred marks you had saved from your work, real work, you got five. So this trauma is very deep in German minds, even in mine, in every German. What will become of what you have worked for? Money is work, you know, even for an author. Give me a cigarette.

Vonnegut: Give me half a loaf of bread and I will.

Bibliography

1. CRISIS? WHAT CRISIS?
Umberto Eco, *The Name of The Rose*, Secker & Warburg 1983.
  Reflections On The Name Of The Rose, Secker, 1985.
  Faith In Fakes, Secker 1986.

Stuart Hall et al, *Policing The Crisis*, MacMillan 1978.

Stuart Hall, *Drifting Into A Law And Order Society*,
  The Cobden Lecture 1979 (Available from The Cobden Trust).

Stuart Hall and Martin Jacques (co-ed.),
  The Politics of Thatcherism, Lawrence & Wishart 1983.

2. WRITERS & POLITICS
Nadine Gordimer, *Burger's Daughter*, Penguin 1979.
  July's People, Penguin 1981

Susan Sontag, *Against Interpretation*, Eyre & Spottiswoode, 1967
  Something Out There, Eyre & Spottiswoode, 1967.
  Under The Sign Of Saturn, Writers & Readers 1983.

3. THE NEW COLD WAR
Noam Chomsky and Edward S. Herman,
  The Political Economy of Human Rights, (2 vols.), Spokesman 1979.

Noam Chomsky, *Towards A New Cold War*, Sinclair & Brown 1982.
  Turning The Tide, Pluto 1986.

Fred Halliday and Maxine Molyneux,
  The Ethiopian Revolution, Verso 1982.

Fred Halliday, *The Making Of The 2nd Cold War*, Verso 1983.

E.P. Thompson (ed.), *Exterminism & The New Cold War*, Verso 1982.

4. A NEW EUROPE?
George Konrad, *Antipolitics* Quartet 1984.
  The Loser, King Penguin 1985.

E.P. Thompson, *Zero Option*, Merlin 1982.
   The Heavy Dancers, Merlin 1985.
   Double Exposure, Merlin 1985.

E.P. Thompson & Dan Smith (co-ed.)
   Protest And Survive, Penguin 1980.

5. WRITING FOR A FUTURE

Günter Grass, *Dog Years,* Penguin 1963.
   The Tin Drum, Penguin 1959.
   On Writing & Politics, 1967-83, Secker 1985.
   The Rat, Secker 1987.

Salman Rushdie, *Midnight's Children*, Picador 1981.
   Shame, Picador 1983.
   The Jaguar's Smile, Picador 1987.

6. WHAT BECAME OF THE BOYS?

Heninrich Böll, *Group Portrait With A Lady*, Penguin 1971.
   The Lost Honour Of Katherina Blum, Penguin 1971.
   What's To Become Of The Boy?, Secker 1985.

Kurt Vonnegut, *Mother Night*, Granada 1961.
   Slaughterhouse Five, Granada 1969.
   Palm Sunday, Granada 1981.

NB. All dates are of original publication; publishers are of original publications or most easily available paperback edition.